A Primer Of The History Of Mathematics

A PRIMER

OF THE

History of Mathematics

BY

W. W. ROUSE BALL

FELLOW AND TUTOR OF TRINITY COLLEGE, CAMBRIDGE.

London

Macmillan & Co.

and New York

1895

TABLE OF CONTENTS.

HISTORY OF MATHEMATICS.

Introductory.

1. Object of this Primer. The object of this primer
is to give a popular account of the history of mathematics,
including therein some notice of the lives and surround-
ings of those to whom its development is mainly due,
as well as of their discoveries. Such a sketch, written
in non-technical language and confined to less than 140
pages, can contain nothing beyond a bare outline of the
subject, and of course is not intended for those to whom
it is familiar. But to any unacquainted with the leading
facts here given, I hope even a sketch like this may prove
not uninteresting; while to those (teachers or learners),
who have no time to read larger works, but who hold, as
I do, that a knowledge of the history of a science lends
interest to its study and often increases its educational
value, I trust that this primer may be of some use. For
references to the authorities employed and for fuller
details, I refer the reader to my *History of Mathematics*
(see below, p. 147).

2. Arrangement of this Primer. The history of
mathematics cannot with certainty be traced back to
any school or period before that of the Ionian Greeks,
but the subsequent history may be divided into periods,
the distinctions between which are tolerably well marked.

A

I shall first discuss the history of mathematics under Greek influence (arts. 3 to 94), then the mathematics of the middle ages and the renaissance (arts. 95 to 184), then the introduction of modern analysis (arts. 185 to 281), and, lastly, the leading features of recent mathematics (arts. 282 to 319).

Mathematics under Greek Influence.

3. Egyptian and Phoenician Mathematics. There can be no doubt that most early races which have left records knew something of numeration and mechanics, and that a few were also acquainted with the elements of land-surveying. In particular, the Egyptians paid attention to geometry and numbers, and probably the Phoenicians to practical arithmetic, book-keeping, navigation, and may-be land-surveying. The results attained by these people seem to have been accessible, under certain conditions, to travellers; and to the interest excited by various geometrical propositions thus communicated by the Egyptian priests in the seventh century before Christ we may ascribe the commencement of the study of mathematics by the Greeks. It is probable that the knowledge of the Egyptians and Phoenicians was largely the result of observation and measurement, and represented the accumulated experience of many ages. On the other hand, Greek mathematics, which originated with the study of geometry, tended from its commencement to be deductive and scientific.

4. Thales, circ. 640-550 B.C. The founder of the earliest Greek school of mathematics and philosophy was Thales of Miletus. The first part of his life was spent in commerce and in public affairs, where he had a considerable reputation for shrewdness and sagacity: thus, to take one instance, when in one year there was a prospect of an unusually abundant crop of olives, he got possession of all the olive-presses of the district, and, having thus "cornered" them, was able to make his own terms for lending them out. In his youth, his business took him to Egypt, and there, during his leisure, he studied astronomy and geometry. When he was middle-aged, he abandoned business, settled at Miletus, and devoted himself for the rest of his life to the study of philosophy and science.

5. It is believed that Thales presented his geometrical teaching in the form of isolated propositions not arranged in a logical sequence, but that the proofs were deductive, so that the theorems were not a mere induction from a large number of special instances as probably had been the case with the Egyptians. The deductive character which he thus gave to the science is his chief claim to distinction.

6. The following comprise the chief propositions that can with reasonable probability be attributed to him.

(i) The angles at the base of an isosceles triangle are equal (Euc. I. 5). Not improbably this was proved by taking another exactly equal isosceles triangle, turning it over, and then superposing it on the first.

(ii) If two straight lines cut one another, the vertically opposite angles are equal (Euc. I. 15). Most likely Thales regarded this as axiomatic.

(iii) A triangle is determined if its base and base angles be given (cf. Euc. I. 26). Apparently this was applied to find the distance of a ship at sea; the base being a tower, and the base angles being obtained by observation.

(iv) The sides of equiangular triangles are proportionals (Euc. VI. 4, or VI. 2). This may have been suggested by a desire to find the height of a pyramid, for in a dialogue given by Plutarch, the speaker, addressing Thales, says, "placing your stick at the end of the shadow of the pyramid, you made by the sun's rays two triangles, and so proved that the [height of the] pyramid was to the [length of the] stick as the shadow of the pyramid to the shadow of the stick." The Egyptians are said to have been previously ignorant of the theorem, and to have been amazed at this novel application of abstract science.

(v) The angle subtended by a diameter of a circle at any point in the circumference is a· right angle (Euc. III. 31). It is said that Thales proved this by joining the centre of the circle to the apex of the angle, thus forming two isosceles triangles, and then applied the property (i) above. If this account of his proof be correct, he must have been aware that the sum of the angles of a triangle is equal to two right angles. It is not unlikely that this proposition was suggested by the tiles used in paving floors, and was proved first for particular cases and then generally as follows. Any two equal right-angled triangles can be placed in juxtaposition so as to form a rectangle, the sum of whose angles is four right angles, hence the proposition is true for any right-angled triangle. But any triangle can be split into two right-angled triangles by drawing a perpendicular from the biggest angle on the opposite side, and therefore the proposition is true generally.

7. Among his contemporaries, Thales was more famous as an astronomer than as a geometrician. Without going into details it may be mentioned that he taught that the earth was spherical, and that a year contained about 365 days. He seems to have explained the causes of the eclipses both of the sun and moon, and it is well known that he predicted a solar eclipse which took place at or about the time he foretold: the actual date was May 28, 585 B.C. But though this prophecy and its fulfilment gave extraordinary prestige to his teaching, and secured him the name of one of the seven sages of Greece, it is probable that he only made use of one of

the Egyptian or Chaldean registers which stated that solar eclipses recur at intervals of 18 years 11 days.

8. **Successors of Thales.** The school established by Thales continued to flourish for more than a century after his death, but as time went on its members devoted most of their attention to philosophy and astronomy. The further advance of Greek mathematics was made chiefly under the influence of the Pythagoreans, who created a science of numbers in addition to developing that of geometry.

9. **Pythagoras, circ. 569-500 B.C.** Pythagoras spent the early years of his manhood in study and travel in Asia Minor and Egypt, finally settling at his birthplace, Samos, where he lectured, though with no special success. About 529 B.C. he migrated to Sicily; thence he went to Tarentum; but shortly moved to Croton, in the south of Italy. Here the schools that he opened were crowded with an enthusiastic audience; citizens of all ranks, especially those of the upper classes, attended, and even the women broke a law which forbade their going to public meetings and flocked to hear him.

10. Pythagoras divided those who attended his lectures into two classes, whom we may term probationers and Pythagoreans. The majority were probationers, but it was only to the Pythagoreans that his chief discoveries were revealed. The latter formed a brotherhood with all things in common, holding the same philosophical and political beliefs, engaged in the same pursuits, and bound by oath not to reveal the teaching or secrets of the school; their food was simple; their discipline severe; and their mode of life arranged to encourage self-command, temperance, purity, and obedience. This strict discipline and secret organization gave the society a temporary supremacy in the state which brought on it the hatred of various classes; and finally, instigated by his political opponents, the mob murdered Pythagoras and many of his followers.

Though the political influence of the Pythagoreans was thus destroyed, they seem to have re-established themselves at once as a philosophical and mathematical society, with Tarentum as their head-quarters. They continued to flourish for more than a hundred years, but to the end they remained a secret society, and we are therefore in ignorance of the details of their history.

11. Pythagoras did not allow the use of text-books, and the assumption of his school was that all their knowledge was held in common and veiled from the outside world. Gradually, as the society became more scattered, this rule was abandoned, and treatises containing the substance of their teaching and doctrines were written. The first book of the kind was composed by Philolaus (circ. 385 B.C.), and we are told that Plato secured a copy of it.

12. Pythagoras was primarily a philosopher and moralist, but his philosophical and ethical teaching were preceded by and were founded on a study of mathematics, which he classified under four heads. This "quadrivium" consisted of magnitudes at rest or geometry, magnitudes in motion or astronomy (and perhaps mechanics), numbers absolute or arithmetic, and numbers applied or music. This classification continued in use for several centuries.

13. Pythagoras made geometry the foundation of his teaching; moreover, he impressed on it that deductive character which it still possesses, and there is reason to believe that he arranged the leading propositions in a logical order. He himself probably knew and taught the substance of what is contained in the first two books of Euclid, and was acquainted with a few other isolated theorems including some elementary propositions on irrational magnitudes (while his successors added several of the propositions in the sixth and eleventh books of Euclid); but it is thought that many of his proofs were

not rigorous, and in particular that the converse of a theorem was sometimes assumed without a proof.

14. Of his own discoveries, I may mention the following.

(i) The demonstration given in Euc. I. 32 that the sum of the angles of a triangle is equal to two right angles. In it, the results of the propositions Euc. I. 13 and the first part of Euc. I. 29 are quoted, and it is most likely that the proofs given by Euclid of the two propositions last mentioned are also due to Pythagoras.

(ii) The properties of right-angled triangles which are given in Euc. I. 47 and I. 48. We know that the proofs of these propositions which are found in Euclid were of Euclid's own invention, and the demonstrations of Pythagoras are not now extant.

(iii) Pythagoras is also credited with the theorems Euc. I. 44 and I. 45, and with giving a solution of the problem Euc. II. 14. It is said that on the discovery of the construction for this problem he sacrificed an ox, but as his school had all things in common his liberality was more apparent than real.

(iv) Pythagoras enumerated as regular solids the cube, the tetrahedron, the octrahedron, and perhaps the iscosahedron, to which Hippasus (circ. 470 B.C.), a member of his school, added the dodecahedron.

(v) It would seem that Pythagoras was acquainted with some properties of irrational magnitudes. In particular it is believed that he proved that the side and the diagonal of a square are incommensurable; and that it was this discovery which led the Greeks to banish from their geometry the conceptions of number and measurement. It is not unlikely that his proof was as follows. If possible let the side be to the diagonal in a commensurable ratio, namely, that of the two integers a and b. Suppose this ratio reduced to its lowest terms so that a and b have no common divisor other than unity, that is, they are prime to one another. Then (by Euc. I. 47) $b^2 = 2a^2$; therefore

b^2 is an even number; therefore b is an even number; hence, since a is prime to b, a must be an odd number. Again, since it has been shown that b is an even number, b may be represented by $2n$; therefore $(2n)^2 = 2a^2$; therefore $a^2 = 2n^2$; therefore a^2 is an even number; therefore a is an even number. Thus the same number a must be both odd and even, which is absurd; therefore the side and diagonal are incommensurable.

15. Pythagoras may be said to have created the science of numbers or higher arithmetic; this was regarded by his school as one of his chief glories. He attached great importance to it, for knowing that measurement was essential to the accurate definition of form, he thought that it was also to some extent the cause of form, and therefore he taught that the foundation of the theory of the universe was to be found in the science of numbers. It must be remembered, however, that this Greek "arithmetic" had no connection with the art of calculation,* but was concerned only with properties of numbers (such as proportions, factors, series, etc.), and that these properties were often investigated by the aid of geometry.

16. Pythagoras commenced his theory of arithmetic by dividing all numbers into even or odd. He further classified them into primes or composites, dividing the latter

---

* In Greek times and long afterwards, the simpler processes of calculation and of mercantile arithmetic were performed chiefly by the use of the *abacus*. In its simplest form this consists of a wooden board with a number of grooves cut in it, or of a table covered with sand in which grooves are made with the fingers: to represent a number, as many pebbles or beads are put on the first groove as there are units, as many on the second as there are tens, and so on. When by its aid a number of objects were counted, for each object a pebble was put on the first groove; and as soon as there were ten pebbles there, they were taken off and one pebble put on the second groove; and so on. It was sometimes made by fastening on a frame a number of parallel strings on which beads could be threaded. Thus the abacus provided a concrete way of representing a number in the decimal system of notation.

into three species according as they were greater than, equal to, or less than the sum of their integral factors. He also discussed numbers of specified forms, particularly "triangular" numbers of the form $\frac{1}{2}n(n+1)$, and triplets of integers like 3, 4, 5 ; or 5, 12, 13 ; (or generally like $m^2 - n^2$, $2mn$, $m^2 + n^2$, where m and n are integers), which can represent the sides of a right-angled triangle. Another class of problems dealt with numbers which form a proportion. Lastly, the Pythagoreans were concerned with series of numbers in arithmetical, geometrical, harmonical, and musical progressions. The three progressions first mentioned are well known ; four integers are said to be in musical progression when they are in the ratio $a : 2ab/(a+b) : \frac{1}{2}(a+b) : b$.

17. The Pythagorean treatment of the other subjects in the quadrivium, and the philosophical ideas based on these mathematical researches, require no mention here.

18. **The Fifth Century B.C.** After the death of Pythagoras, mathematics continued to be studied by various Greek philosophers who belonged to his school, or were directly influenced by it. In particular, I may mention Oenopides, Parmenides, Zeno, Archytas, Theodorus, Bryso, Antipho, and Hippias, as prominent teachers of the fifth century.

19. *Oenopides* of Chios is credited with the solution of the problems to draw a straight line from a given external point perpendicular to a given straight line (Euc. I. 12), and at a given point to construct an angle equal to a given angle (Euc. I. 23).

20. *Parmenides* and *Zeno* of Elea were celebrated for some paradoxical propositions on motion, notably the fallacy of Achilles and the tortoise. The argument was that even if Achilles ran ten times as fast as a tortoise, yet if the tortoise had a start of (say) 1000 yards it could never be overtaken : for, when Achilles had gone the 1000 yards, the tortoise would still be 100 yards in front of him ; by the time he had covered these 100 yards, it would

still be 10 yards in front of him ; and so on for ever : thus Achilles would get nearer and nearer to the tortoise but never overtake it—a conclusion which obviously is false.

21. *Archytas* of Tarentum was recognized as head of the Pythagorean school about 400 B.C. He is said to have applied geometry to the investigation of mechanical questions. His work on this subject is not now extant, but it is probable that it suffered from the common Greek fault of not sufficiently resting the study of science on the results of observation and experiment. Archytas is also known for his geometrical solution of one of the most famous problems of antiquity, namely, to find the side of a cube whose volume is double that of a given cube. In it he made use of curves drawn in space, and shewed himself acquainted with the results of the propositions, Euc. III. 18, III. 35, and XI. 19.

22. Another Pythagorean of about the same date was *Theodorus* of Cyrene, who is believed to have proved geometrically that the numbers represented by $\sqrt{3}$, $\sqrt{5}$, $\sqrt{6}$, $\sqrt{7}$, $\sqrt{8}$, $\sqrt{10}$, $\sqrt{11}$, $\sqrt{12}$, $\sqrt{13}$, $\sqrt{14}$, $\sqrt{15}$, and $\sqrt{17}$ are incommensurable with unity.

23. His contemporaries *Bryso* and *Antipho* are noticeable for their attempt to find the area of a circle by considering it as the limit of an inscribed regular polygon having a very large number of sides.

24. Finally, I may mention *Hippias* of Elis, who invented a curve called the quadratrix, by which an angle can be trisected, or indeed divided in any required ratio.

25. **Rise of the Athenian School.** Towards the close of the fifth century B.C., Athens became the chief centre of mathematical studies. Several causes conspired to bring this about. During that century she had become, partly by commerce, partly by appropriating for her own purposes the contributions of her allies, the most wealthy city in Greece; and the genius of her statesmen had

made her the centre on which the politics of the peninsula turned. Moreover, whatever states disputed her claim to political supremacy, her intellectual pre-eminence was admitted by all, and there was no school of philosophy which had not at some time in that century been represented at Athens by one or more of its leading thinkers.

The history of the Athenian school begins with the teaching of Hippocrates about 420 B.C.; the school was established on a permanent basis by the labours of Plato and Eudoxus; and, together with the neighbouring school of Cyzicus (which was founded by Eudoxus, and closely connected with that of Athens), continued to extend on the lines laid down by these geometricians until the foundation (about 300 B.C.) of the university at Alexandria drew thither most of the talent of Greece.

26. **Hippocrates, circ. 420 B.C.** Hippocrates was a merchant of Chios, who came to Athens about 430 B.C. to try to recover some property of which he had been defrauded by certain citizens of that city. He seems to have failed in his suit, but while prosecuting it he attended various lectures, and finally (in all probability to earn a livelihood) opened a school of geometry.

27. Hippocrates wrote the earliest text-book on geometry. In it, it is believed, he commenced the custom of using letters to describe points in a diagram, and first drew attention to the method of "reducing" one theorem to another, which, being proved, the thing proposed necessarily follows, of which the *reductio ad absurdum* is a particular case. He may be said to have introduced the geometry of the circle. He discovered that similar segments of a circle contain equal angles; that the angle subtended by the chord of a circle is greater than, equal to, or less than a right angle as the segment of the circle containing it is less than, equal to, or greater than a semicircle (Euc. III. 31); and probably

several other of the propositions in the third book of
Euclid. It is most likely that he also established the
propositions that circles are to one another as the squares
of their diameters (Euc. XII. 2), and that similar segments are as the squares of their chords.

28. The most celebrated discoveries of Hippocrates
were, however, in connection with *the quadrature of the
circle* and *the duplication of the cube,* and owing to his
influence these problems played a prominent part in the
history of the Athenian school.

29. The quadrature of a circle (that is, the construction
of a square whose area is equal to that of a circle) is
insoluble by elementary geometry. But in his efforts,
necessarily vain, to find a solution, Hippocrates discovered
various theorems connected with *lunes*: these are interesting as being the earliest known instances in which areas
bounded by curves were determined.

The following proposition will illustrate his method.
Let ABC be an isosceles right-angled triangle inscribed
in the semicircle $ABOC$ whose centre is O and diameter
BC. On AB and AC as diameters, and on the sides
remote from O, describe semicircles. Then, we have

$BC^2 = AB^2 + AC^2$ (Euc. I. 47); therefore, by Euc. XII. 2,

area $\frac{1}{2} \odot$ on BC = sum of areas of $\frac{1}{2} \odot$s on AB and AC.

Take away the common parts

$\therefore$ area $\triangle ABC$ = sum of areas of lunes on AB and AC.

Hence the area of one of these lunes is equal to half that
of the triangle ABC.

30. The other problem to which Hippocrates paid special
attention was the duplication of a cube, that is, the determination of the side of a cube whose volume is double
that of a given cube. He reduced the difficulty to that
of finding two means between one straight line (a) and
another twice as long ($2a$). If these means be x and y,
we have $a : x = x : y = y : 2a$, from which it follows that
$x^3 = 2a^3$.

31. **Plato**, 429-348 B.C. The next philosopher of the Athenian school who requires mention here is Plato. After the execution of Socrates in 399 B.C., Plato spent some years in travel, and studied mathematics in the Pythagorean schools. He returned to Athens about 380 B.C., and formed a school of his own in a suburban gymnasium called the "Academy." Like Pythagoras, Plato was primarily a philosopher, and held that the secret of the universe was to be found in number and in form; hence he made a study of geometry or some exact science an indispensable preliminary to that of philosophy. The inscription over the entrance to his school ran "let none ignorant of geometry enter my door," and on one occasion an applicant who knew no geometry is said to have been refused admission as a student.

32. It is probably due to Plato that subsequent geometricians began the subject with a carefully compiled series of definitions, postulates, and axioms. He systematized the methods which could be used in attacking mathematical questions, and in particular directed attention to the value of analysis. The analytical method of proof begins by assuming that the theorem or problem is solved, and thence deducing some result; if the result be false, the theorem is not true or the problem is incapable of solution: if the result be known to be true, and if the steps be reversible, we get (by reversing them) a synthetic proof; but if the steps be not reversible, no conclusion can be drawn.

33. An extant instance of a mathematical theorem attributable to Plato is the following. If CAB and DAB be two right-angled triangles, having one side, AB, common, their other sides, AD and BC, parallel, and their hypothenuses, AC and BD, at right angles, then, if these hypothenuses cut in P, we have $PC : PB = PB : PA = PA : PD$. This theorem was used in duplicating the cube, for, if such triangles can be constructed having $PD = 2PC$, the problem

will be solved.   It is easy to make an instrument by which
the triangles can be constructed mechanically.

34. **Eudoxus, 408-355 B.C.** Of Eudoxus, the third
great mathematician of the Athenian school and the
founder of that at Cyzicus, we know little, except that
he also studied under the Pythagoreans.   His work seems
to have been of a high order of excellence.

35. Eudoxus discovered most of what is printed in the
fifth book of Euclid, and proved it in the way there given.
The division of a line in extreme and mean ratio is effected
in Euc. II. 11 ; Eudoxus established the theorems on a line
so divided which were inserted by Euclid at the commencement of his thirteenth book.   Eudoxus further established
the "method of exhaustions"; which depends on the proposition that "if from the greater of two unequal magnitudes
there be taken more than its half, and from the remainder
more than its half, and so on ; there will at length remain
a magnitude less than the least of the proposed magnitudes" (Euc. x. 1).   By the aid of this theorem the ancient
geometers were able to avoid.the use of infinitesimals.   The
method is rigorous, but awkward of application : an illustration of its use is to be found in the demonstration of
Euc. XII. 2, namely, that the square of the radius of one
circle is to the square of the radius of another circle as the
area of the first circle is to an area which is neither less
nor greater than the area of the second circle, and which
therefore must be exactly equal to it : the proof given by
Euclid is (as was usual) completed by a *reductio ad absurdum.*
Eudoxus applied the principle to shew that the volume
of a pyramid (or a cone) is one-third that of the prism (or
cylinder) on the same base and of the same altitude
(Euc. XII. 7 and 10).

36. Eudoxus constructed an orrery, and wrote a treatise
on astronomy, in which he adopted the hypothesis that the
sun, moon, and stars were respectively attached to moving spheres, which by their rotation produced the effects

observed. In all he required twenty-seven spheres. As observations became more accurate, subsequent astronomers who accepted the theory had continually to introduce fresh spheres to make the theory agree with the facts.

37. **Menaechmus, circ. 375-325 B.C.** Menaechmus, who was a pupil of Eudoxus, and probably succeeded him as head of the school at Cyzicus, had a great reputation as a teacher, and consequently was appointed tutor to Alexander the Great. In answer to his pupil's request to make his proofs shorter, he made the well-known reply that though in the country there are private and even royal roads, yet in geometry there is only one road for all.

38. Menaechmus was the first to discuss the conic sections, which were long called the Menaechmian triads. He divided them into three classes, and investigated their properties, not by taking different plane sections of a fixed cone, but by keeping his plane fixed and cutting it by different cones. He shewed that the section of a right cone by a plane perpendicular to a generator is an ellipse, if the cone be acute-angled; a parabola, if it be right-angled; and a hyperbola, if it be obtuse-angled.

39. He also pointed out how conics could be used in either of two ways to give a solution of the problem to duplicate a cube. In the first of these, he shewed that two parabolas having a common vertex, axes at right angles, and such that the latus rectum of the one is double that of the other will intersect in another point whose abscissa (or ordinate) will give a solution: for (using analysis) if the equations of the parabolas be $y^2 = 2ax$ and $x^2 = ay$, they intersect in a point whose abscissa is given by $x^3 = 2a^3$. It is probable that this method was suggested by the form in which Hippocrates had cast the problem: namely, to find x and y so that $a : x = x : y = y : 2a$, whence we have $x^2 = ay$ and $y^2 = 2ax$.

The second solution given by Menaechmus was of a similar kind, but depended on finding the points of intersection of a parabola and a rectangular hyperbola.

40. **Aristaeus** and **Theaetetus.** Of the other members of these schools, Aristaeus and Theaetetus deserve mention. Their works are lost, but we know that Aristaeus wrote on the five regular solids and on conic sections, and that Theaetetus developed the theory of incommensurable magnitudes. The only theorem we can now definitely ascribe to the latter is that given in Euc. x. 9, namely, that the squares on two commensurable right lines have one to the other a ratio which a square number has to a square number (and conversely); but the squares on two incommensurable right lines have one to the other a ratio which cannot be expressed as that of a square number to a square number (and conversely).

41. **Close of the Athenian School.** The contemporaries or successors of the mathematicians named above wrote some fresh text-books on the elements of geometry and the conic sections, introduced problems concerned with finding loci, and efficiently carried out the work commenced by Plato of systematizing the knowledge already acquired, but they originated no new methods of research.

42. **The First Alexandrian School.** The earliest attempt to found a university, as we understand the word, was made at Alexandria. It was the creation of Ptolemy, who, on the death of Alexander the Great in 323 B.C. and the division of his empire, secured Egypt, and chose Alexandria as the capital of his kingdom. It was Ptolemy's policy to attract learned men to the city, and to further this he established a university in immediate proximity to his palace. Richly endowed, and amply supplied with lecture-rooms, libraries, museums, laboratories, gardens, and all the plant and machinery

that ingenuity could suggest, it became the metropolis
of Greek learning, and remained so for a thousand years.
Of its internal organization and discipline we know little.
It was particularly fortunate in securing or producing
within the first century of its existence three of the
greatest mathematicians of antiquity—Euclid, Archimedes,
and Apollonius : they laid down the lines on which mathematics was subsequently studied; and, largely owing to
their influence, the history of mathematics centres more
or less round that of Alexandria until the destruction of
the city by the Arabs in 641 A.D. For this reason the
Alexandrian schools are commonly taken to include all
Greek mathematicians of their time.

43. **Euclid, circ. 330-275 B.C.** Of Euclid's life
we know next to nothing save that he was of Greek
descent, was probably educated at Athens, and lectured
at Alexandria, from the foundation of the university
about the year 300 B.C. until his death. We find that
the saying that there is no royal road in geometry was
attributed to Euclid as well as to Menaechmus, but it
is an obvious epigram. Euclid is also said to have insisted that knowledge was worth acquiring for its own
sake, and we are told that when a lad who had just
begun geometry asked "what do I gain by learning all
this stuff?" Euclid made his slave give the boy some
coppers, "since," said he, "he must make a profit out
of what he learns." The Arabian writers, who may
perhaps convey to us the traditions of Alexandria, represent him as a gentle and kindly old man.

44. Euclid was the author of several works, but his
reputation rests mainly on his *Elements*. This treatise
contains a systematic exposition of the leading propositions of elementary geometry (exclusive of conic sections)
and of the theory of numbers. It was at once adopted
by the Greeks as the standard text-book on the elements
of pure mathematics. The bulk of the tenth book seems

B

to have been original, but most of the rest was a compilation from the works of previous writers, though this material was re-arranged, and in some cases new proofs substituted.

The way in which the propositions are proved, consisting of enunciation, statement, construction, proof, and conclusion are due to Euclid; so also is the synthetical character of the work, each proof being written out as a logically correct train of reasoning, but without any clue being given to the method by which it was obtained.

45. The geometrical parts of the *Elements* are so well known that I need only allude to them. The first four books and book VI deal with plane geometry; the theory of proportion is discussed in book V; and books XI and XII treat of solid geometry. The results of the fifth book apply to any magnitudes, and therefore are true of numbers as well as of geometrical magnitudes. This fact was familiar to the Greeks, thus it is probable (to take a particular instance) that they were aware that Euc. VI. 28, 29, contain geometrical solutions of the quadratic equations $ax^2 \mp bx \pm c = 0$, where a, b, c, denote numbers.

46. In books VII, VIII, and IX Euclid discussed the theory of rational numbers. In the seventh book he shewed that if, in the usual process for finding the greatest common measure of two numbers, the last divisor be unity, the numbers must be prime; and he thence deduced the rule for finding their G.C.M. He next dealt with fractions. He then discussed prime numbers. He concluded with some propositions on the least common multiple of numbers. The eighth book is chiefly devoted to numbers in continued proportion, *i.e.*, in a geometrical progression. In the ninth book Euclid continued the discussion of geometrical progressions. He also developed the theory of primes, shewed that the number of primes is infinite, and discussed some properties of odd and even

numbers. He concluded by shewing how to construct a "perfect" number.

47. In the tenth book Euclid treated of irrational magnitudes; and, since the Greeks possessed no symbolism for surds, he was forced to adopt a geometrical representation. He commenced with some theorems on incommensurable magnitudes, and then went on to discuss all lines which can be represented by $\sqrt{(\sqrt{a} \pm \sqrt{b})}$, where a and b denote commensurable magnitudes.

48. In addition to the *Elements*, Euclid published two collections of geometrical problems, a book on conic sections, a work on the cone and cylinder, and a treatise on porisms. He also wrote on geometrical optics and geometrical astronomy. Throughout his writings he dealt with magnitudes rather than with their numerical measures.

49. **Aristarchus, 310-250 B.C.** Aristarchus of Samos is worthy of mention here because he asserted that the sun was the centre of the universe, and that the earth revolved round the sun. This view, in spite of the simple explanation it afforded of various phenomena, was rejected by most of his contemporaries. But his propositions on the sizes and distances of the sun and moon were correct in principle, though the inaccurate measurements on which they were based vitiated his numerical conclusions, which were, however, generally accepted as approximately correct. He estimated the distance of the sun to be about 5×10^9 stadia.

50. **Archimedes, 287-212 B.C.** The works of Aristarchus and other writers of this time have been completely overshadowed by the reputation of Archimedes, whose marvellous mathematical powers have been surpassed only by those of Newton. Archimedes, who probably was related to the royal family at Syracuse, was educated at Alexandria, but as soon as he had finished his studies, returned to Sicily where he passed the remainder of his life.

51. Archimedes, like Plato, held that it was no part of the duty of a philosopher to apply science to practical uses; but, in spite of this view, he introduced a large number of new inventions. The stories of the detection of the fraudulent goldsmith and of the use of burning glasses to destroy the ships of the Roman blockading squadron will recur to most readers. Perhaps it is not as well known that Hiero, who had built a ship so large that he could not launch it off the slips, applied to Archimedes, who overcame the difficulty by means of cogwheels worked by an endless screw. It is said that it was on this occasion, in acknowledging the compliments of Hiero, that Archimedes made the well-known remark that had he but a fixed fulcrum he could move the earth.

52. Most mathematicians are aware that the Archimedean screw was another of his inventions. It consists of a tube, open at both ends, and bent into the form of a spiral like a cork-screw. If one end be immersed in water, and the instrument be turned round its axis (which must be inclined to the vertical at an angle greater than the pitch of the screw), then the water will flow along the tube and out at the other end. It was used in Egypt to drain the fields after an inundation of the Nile, and was also applied by the ancients to remove water from the hold of a ship.

53. Archimedes further devised the catapults which kept the Romans, who were besieging Syracuse, at bay for a considerable time. These were constructed so that the range could be made either short or long at pleasure, and so that they could be discharged through a small loophole without exposing the artillerymen to the fire of the enemy. So effective did they prove that the siege was turned into a blockade, and three years elapsed before the town was taken (212 B.C.).

54. Archimedes was killed during the sack of the city which followed its capture, in spite of special orders that his house and life should be spared. The Romans engraved

on his tomb (in accordance with a wish he had expressed)
the figure of a sphere inscribed in a cylinder, in com-
memoration of the proof he had given that the volume of
a sphere is equal to two-thirds that of the circumscribing
right cylinder, and its surface to four times the area of a
great circle.

55. It is difficult to explain in a concise form the works
or discoveries of Archimedes, partly because he wrote on
nearly all the mathematical subjects then known, and
partly because his writings are contained in a series of
disconnected monographs; but, confining myself to such
works of his as are still extant, I may mention the
following.

(i) His tract on the Measure of the Circle. In this he
first proved that the area is the same as that of a right-
angled triangle, whose sides are equal respectively to the
radius a and the circumference of the circle, $i.e.$ the area is
equal to $\frac{1}{2}a(2\pi a)$. Next he shewed that $\pi a^2 : (2a)^2 = 11 : 14$
very nearly; and then that π is less than $3\frac{1}{7}$ and greater
than $3\frac{10}{71}$: to obtain these limits, he inscribed in and
circumscribed about a circle regular polygons of ninety-six
sides, calculated their perimeters, and assumed the circumference of the circle to lie between them. Of course these
results were proved geometrically.

(ii) The Quadrature of the Parabola. In this Archimedes established some properties of conics, and in particular found the area cut off from a parabola by any chord.

(iii) A work on spirals represented by the equation
$r = c\theta$, wherein most of their properties are investigated.

(iv) His Sphere and Cylinder. In this, which he regarded as his masterpiece, he determined the surface and
volume of a pyramid, of a cone, and of a sphere, as well
as of the figures produced by the revolution of polygons
inscribed in a circle about a diameter of the circle.

(v) His Conoids and Spheroids, wherein he discussed
quadrics of revolution and investigated their volumes.

(vi) On arithmetic Archimedes wrote two papers. The object of the first paper (which is now lost) had been to suggest a convenient system by which numbers of any magnitude could be represented in a kind of decimal notation. The second paper was to shew that the method enabled one to write any number however large; and to illustrate the power of his method he found a superior limit to the number of grains of sand which would fill the whole universe, *i.e.* a sphere whose centre is the earth, and radius the distance of the sun for which he accepted the estimate of Aristarchus. His result is that the number of grains of sand required to fill the universe is less than 10^{63}. Probably this system of numeration was suggested merely as a scientific curiosity.

(vii) His Mechanics is a work on statics with special reference to the equilibrium of plane laminas and to properties of their centres of gravity.

(viii) His work on floating bodies was the first attempt to apply mathematical reasoning to hydrostatics. The story of the manner in which his attention was directed to the subject is told by Vitruvius. Hiero, the king of Syracuse, had given some gold to a goldsmith to make into a crown. The crown was delivered, made up, and of the proper weight, but it was suspected that the workman had appropriated some of the gold, replacing it by an equal weight of silver. Archimedes was there-upon consulted. Shortly afterwards, when in the public baths, he noticed that his body was pressed upwards by a force which increased the more completely he was immersed in the water. Recognizing the value of the observation, he rushed out and ran home through the streets, shouting "I have found it, I have found it." There (to follow a later account) on making accurate experiments he found that when equal weights of gold and silver were weighed in water they no longer appeared equal: each seemed lighter than before by the weight of the water it displaced, and as the silver was more bulky than the gold its weight was more diminished. Hence, if on a balance he weighed the crown against an equal weight of gold and then immersed the whole in water, the gold would outweigh the crown if any silver had been used in its construction. Tradition says that the goldsmith was found to be fraudulent.

56. As an illustration of the power of Archimedes I may mention that the science of statics rested on his theory of the lever until 1586, when Stevinus published his treatise on statics; and no distinct advance was made in the theory of hydrostatics until Stevinus in the same work investigated the laws which regulate the pressure of fluids (see below, art. 173). In the old and medieval world Archimedes was unanimously reckoned as the first of mathematicians: and perhaps in the modern world Newton alone can be considered as his equal or superior.

57. **Apollonius, circ. 260-200 B.C.** Another distinguished mathematician of the third century B.C. was Apollonius of Perga. We know little of him beyond the fact that he studied in Alexandria for many years, and probably lectured there for some time. He then moved to Pergamum, where a university had been established in imitation of that at Alexandria. Ultimately he returned to Alexandria, and lived there till his death, which was nearly contemporaneous with that of Archimedes. He is described as "vain, jealous of the reputation of others, and ready to seize every opportunity to depreciate them."

58. In his great treatise on geometrical conic sections he so thoroughly investigated the properties of these curves that he left but little for his successors to add. This work was accepted at once as the standard text-book on the subject, and completely superseded the treatises of Menaechmus, Aristaeus, and Euclid. It was divided into eight books. Apollonius had no idea of the directrix, and was not aware that the parabola had a

focus, but, with the exception of the propositions which involve these, his first three books contain most of the propositions which are found in modern works. In the fourth book he developed the theory of lines cut harmonically, and treated of the points of intersection of systems of conics. In the fifth book he commenced with the theory of maxima and minima; applied it to find the centre of curvature at any point of a conic, and the evolute of the curve; and discussed the number of normals which can be drawn from a point to a conic. In the sixth book he treated of similar conics. The seventh and eighth books were given up to a discussion of conjugate diameters.

The verbose and tedious explanations make the book repulsive to most modern readers; but the logical arrange-ment and reasoning are unexceptional, and it has been not unfitly described as the crown of Greek geometry.

59. Besides this immense treatise Apollonius wrote numerous tracts on particular geometrical problems, as well as memoirs on arithmetic, astronomy, and the theory of the screw in statics.

60. **Comparison of the Methods of Archimedes and Apollonius.** It has been remarked that the methods used by Archimedes and Apollonius are sharply con-trasted. Archimedes, in attacking the problem of the quadrature of curvilinear areas, established the principles of the geometry which rests on measurements: this naturally gave rise to the infinitesimal calculus, and in fact the method of exhaustions as used by Archimedes does not differ in principle from the method of limits as used by Newton. Apollonius, on the other hand, in investigating the properties of conic sections by means of transversals involving the ratio of rectilineal distances and of perspective, laid the foundations of the geometry of form and position.

61. **Eratosthenes, 275-194 B.C.** Among the con-temporaries of Archimedes and Apollonius I may mention

Eratosthenes. He suggested the calendar (now known as Julian) in which every fourth year contains 366 days; and he determined the obliquity of the ecliptic as 23° 51' 20". He is best known as a geographer: he measured the length of a degree on the earth's surface, making it to be about 79 miles, which is too long by nearly 10 miles, and thence calculated the circumference of the earth to be 252000 stadia, which, if we take the Olympic stadium of 202¼ yards, is equivalent to saying that the radius is about 4600 miles.

Of his work in mathematics we have two extant illustrations: one in a description of an instrument to duplicate a cube, and the other in the rule he gave for constructing a table of prime numbers.

62. **The Second Century before Christ.** The third century before Christ was the most brilliant era in the history of Greek mathematics. But the great mathematicians of that century were geometricians, and under their influence attention was directed almost solely to geometry. Their immediate successors require no notice here, but towards the close of the next century we find two mathematicians who, by turning their attention to new subjects, gave a fresh stimulus to the study of mathematics. These were Hipparchus and Hero.

63. **Hipparchus,. circ. 120 B.C.** Hipparchus was the most eminent of Greek astronomers, his chief predecessors being Eudoxus, Aristarchus, Archimedes, and Eratosthenes. His observations and calculations were far more accurate than those previously published—*ex. gr.* he determined the length of the year to within six minutes of its true value.

64. To account for the lunar motion Hipparchus supposed the moon to move with uniform velocity in a circle, the earth occupying a position near (but not at) the centre of this circle. This is equivalent to saying that the orbit is an epicycle of the first order. The

longitude of the moon obtained on this hypothesis is correct to the first order of small quantities for a few revolutions. To make it correct for any length of time he further supposed that the apse line moved forward about 3° a month, thus giving a correction for evection. He explained the motion of the sun in a similar manner. He commenced a series of observations to enable his successors to account for the planetary motions; and with great perspicacity he predicted that to do this it would be necessary to introduce epicycles of a higher order, that is, to introduce three or more circles, the centre of each successive one moving uniformly on the circumference of the preceding one.

No further advance in the theory of astronomy was made until the time of Copernicus, though the principles laid down by Hipparchus were extended and worked out in detail by Ptolemy.

65. Investigations such as these naturally led to trigonometry, and Hipparchus must be credited with the invention of that subject. It is known that in plane trigonometry he constructed a table of chords of arcs, which is practically the same as one of natural sines; and that in spherical trigonometry he had some method of solving triangles: but his works are lost. I may add that he introduced the conceptions of latitude and longitude as means of defining the position of a place on the earth.

66. **Hero, circ. 120 B.C.** The second of these mathematicians was Hero of Alexandria, who placed engineering and land-surveying on a scientific basis. His strictly mathematical investigations require no special mention, but it may be noticed that he proved that the area of a triangle is equal to $\{s(s-a)(s-b)(s-c)\}^{\frac{1}{2}}$, where s is the semiperimeter, and a, b, c the lengths of the sides; giving as an illustration a triangle whose sides are in the ratio $13 : 14 : 15$.

67. **The First Century before Christ.** The successors of Hipparchus and Hero did not avail themselves of the opportunity thus opened of investigating new subjects, but fell back on the well-worn subject of geometry. The administration of Egypt was definitely undertaken by Rome in 30 B.C. The closing years of the dynasty of the Ptolemies and the earlier years of the Roman occupation of the country were marked by much disorder, civil and political. The studies of the university were naturally interrupted, and it is customary to take this time as the close of the first Alexandrian school.

68. **The Second Alexandrian School.** Although the schools at Alexandria suffered from the disturbances which affected the Roman world in the transition, in fact if not in name, from a republic to an empire, there was no break of continuity; the teaching in the university was never abandoned; and as soon as order was again established students began once more to flock to Alexandria. This time of confusion was, however, contemporaneous with a change in the prevalent views of philosophy which thenceforward were mostly neo-platonic or neo-pythagorean, and it is usually taken as the commencement of a new period.

69. **The First and Second Centuries after Christ.*** Throughout the first century after Christ, geometry continued to be that subject in science to which most attention was devoted, but it was now recognized that the geometry of Archimedes and Apollonius was not capable of much further development. Such geometrical treatises as were produced consisted mostly of commentaries on the writings of the preceding period, while the treatment of the science of numbers became less rigid and more empirical. The second century is chiefly noticeable for the writings of Ptolemy.

* All dates given hereafter are to be taken as *anno domini*, unless the contrary is expressly stated.

70. **Ptolemy.** Ptolemy, who died in 168, was the author of numerous works on mathematics, but is especially famous for his treatises on geography and astronomy. The latter is usually termed the *Almagest*, and it remained a standard authority until the time of Copernicus.

71. The *Almagest* is divided into thirteen books. In the first book Ptolemy discussed various preliminary matters; treated of trigonometry, plane and spherical; gave a table of chords, *i.e.* of natural sines; and explained the obliquity of the ecliptic; in this book he used degrees, minutes, and seconds as measures of angles. The second book is devoted chiefly to phenomena depending on the spherical form of the earth: he remarked that the explanations would be much simplified if the earth were supposed to rotate on its axis once a day, but considered this hypothesis to be inconsistent with known facts. In the third book he explained the motion of the sun round the earth by means of excentrics and epicycles; and in the fourth and fifth books he treated the motion of the moon in a similar way. The sixth book is devoted to the theory of eclipses, and in it he used $3\frac{17}{120}$ as the approximate value of π, which is equivalent to taking π equal to $3 \cdot 1416$. The seventh and eighth books contain a catalogue of 1022 fixed stars determined by indicating those, three or more, that are in the same straight line (this was probably copied from Hipparchus): and in another work Ptolemy added a list of annual sidereal phenomena. The remaining books are given up to the theory of the planets.

72. It is conjectured that the fundamental ideas, the data used, and the explanation of the apparent solar motion were taken from Hipparchus; while the detailed explanations and the calculations of the lunar and planetary motions are due to Ptolemy. The introduction of excentrics and epicycles has been often ridiculed, but if

it be regarded only as a convenient way of expressing known facts, it is legitimate. It was as simple a hypothesis as could be framed to suit the facts then known, and is equivalent to the expression of a given function as a sum of sines or cosines, a method which is of frequent use in modern analysis.

73. The Third Century. Hipparchus and Ptolemy had shewn not only that geometry could be applied to astronomy, but had indicated how new methods of analysis like trigonometry might be thence developed. They found, however, no successors to take up the work commenced so brilliantly, and we must look forward 150 years before we find another geometrician of any eminence.

74. Pappus. Pappus lived and taught at Alexandria about the end of the third century. We know that he had numerous pupils, and it is probable that he temporarily revived an interest in the study of geometry.

75. He wrote several books, but the only one which has come down to us is his Συναγωγή, a collection of Greek mathematical works, together with comments and additional propositions by the editor. A careful comparison of various extant works with the account given of them in this book shews that it is trustworthy, and we rely largely on it for our knowledge of other works now lost. It is not arranged chronologically, but all the treatises on the same subject are grouped together, and it is most likely that it gives roughly the order in which the classical authors were read at Alexandria.

76. The last part of it contains a good deal of original work by Pappus. It would seem that he discovered the focus in the parabola, and the directrix in the conic sections, but in both cases he investigated only a few isolated properties; the earliest comprehensive account of

the foci was given by Kepler, and of the directrix by Newton and Boscovich. In mechanics, Pappus shewed that the centre of gravity of a triangular lamina is the same as that of an inscribed triangular lamina whose vertices divide each of the sides of the original triangle in the same ratio. He also discovered the two theorems which are still quoted in text-books under his name: these are that the volume generated by the revolution of a curve about an axis is equal to the product of the area of the curve and the length of the path described by its centroid, and the surface is equal to the product of the perimeter of the curve and the length of the path described by its centroid.

77. **The Fourth Century.** Throughout the second and third centuries, interest in geometry had steadily decreased, and more attention had been paid to the theory of numbers. It will be remembered that Euclid used lines as symbols for any magnitudes, and investigated theorems about numbers in a strictly scientific manner, but he confined himself to cases where a geometrical representation was possible. Archimedes went further, and introduced numbers into his geometrical discussions. Hero abandoned the geometrical representation of numbers but, as he and other later writers did not succeed in creating any other symbolism for numbers in general, the subject remained much as Archimedes had left it.

78. In the fourth century, however, we begin to come across problems which lead directly to algebraical equations. The following is an example : "Demochares has lived a fourth of his life as a boy; a fifth as a youth; a third as a man; and has spent thirteen years in his dotage : how old is he ?"

79. It is possible that these problems were solved by the method used in similar cases by many medieval writers. This method, usually known as the *rule of false*

assumption, consists in assuming any number for the unknown quantity, and if on trial the given conditions be not satisfied, altering the numbers by a simple proportion as in rule of three. For example, suppose we assume that the age of Demochares is 40, then, by the given conditions, he would have spent $8\frac{2}{3}$ (and not 13) years in his dotage, and therefore we have the ratio of $8\frac{2}{3}$ to 13 equal to the ratio of 40 to his actual age; hence his actual age is 60.

80. But the most recent writers on the subject think that the problems were solved by *rhetorical algebra*, that is, by a process of algebraical reasoning expressed in words and without the use of any symbols.

81. In the midst of this decaying interest in geometry and this commencement of algebraic arithmetic, a single algebraist of marked originality appeared. This was Diophantus, who introduced a system of abbreviations for those operations and quantities which constantly recur, though in using them he observed all the rules of grammatical syntax. The resulting science is called *syncopated algebra*: the demonstrations being given in words at length, except that these abbreviations are used in the text. Broadly speaking, it may be said that European algebra did not advance beyond this stage until the close of the sixteenth century. This introduction of a contraction or a symbol instead of a word to represent an unknown quantity marks a great advance; it is likely enough that it might have been introduced earlier, but for the unlucky system of numeration adopted by the Greeks by which they used all the letters of the alphabet to denote particular numbers and thus made it impossible to employ them to represent any number.

82. Modern algebra has progressed one stage further and is entirely *symbolic*; that is, it has a language of its own, and a system of notation which has no obvious connection with the things represented, while the operations are

performed according to rules distinct from the laws of grammatical construction.

83. Diophantus, circ. 420. All that we know of Diophantus is that he lived at Alexandria, and that most likely he was not a Greek. He wrote a short essay on polygonal numbers; a treatise on algebra which has come down to us in a mutilated condition; and a work on porisms which is lost.

84. In the polygonal numbers Diophantus abandoned the empirical method and reverted to the older system by which numbers are represented by lines, a construction is (if necessary) made, and a strictly deductive proof follows : it may be noticed that in it he quotes propositions, such as Euc. II. 3 and II. 8, as referring to numbers and not to magnitudes.

85. His chief work is his *Arithmetic*, which is really a treatise on algebra ; algebraic symbols are used, the questions are treated analytically, it being tacitly assumed that the steps are reversible ; and the methods are applied to find solutions (though frequently only particular ones) of several problems involving numbers.

86. First, as to the notation of Diophantus. He employed a symbol to represent the unknown quantity in his equations, but as he had only one symbol he could not use more than one unknown at a time. The unknown quantity is usually represented by s. In the plural it is denoted by $\overline{\text{ss}}$ or ss^{ol}. The square of the unknown is called δύναμις, and denoted by δ^v : the cube κύβος, and denoted by κ^v ; and so on up to the sixth power. The coefficients of the unknown quantity and its powers are numbers, and a numerical coefficient is written immediately after the quantity it multiplies ; thus s$\bar{a} = x$, and ss$^{ol}\bar{\iota a} = \overline{\text{ss}}\ \bar{\iota a} = 11x$. An absolute term is regarded as a certain number of units or μονάδες which are represented by μ$^\delta$: thus μ$^\delta\bar{a} = 1$, μ$^\delta\bar{\iota a} = 11$. There is no sign for addition beyond mere juxtaposition. Subtraction is represented by $\pitchfork$, and this symbol

affects all the symbols that follow it. Equality is represented by ι. Thus

$$\kappa^{\hat{\upsilon}}\bar{a} \; \overline{ss}\bar{\eta} \, \pitchfork \, \delta^{\hat{\upsilon}}\bar{\epsilon} \; \mu^{\delta}\bar{a} \; \iota \; \bar{sa}$$

represents $(x^3 + 8x) - (5x^2 + 1) = x,$

87. Next, as to the knowledge of algebra shewn by Diophantus. He commenced with some definitions, and in giving the symbol for *minus* he stated that a subtraction multiplied by a subtraction gives an addition; by this he meant that the product of $-b$ and $-d$ in the expansion of $(a-b)(c-d)$ is $+bd$, but in applying the rule he always took care that the numbers a, b, c, d were so chosen that a is greater than b and c is greater than d. In his solutions of problems he gave rules for solving a simple equation of the first degree and a binomial quadratic. Probably the rule for solving any quadratic equation is in one of the lost books. Most of the work is, however, given up to indeterminate equations: when the equation is of the first degree and between two variables, he assumes a suitable value for one variable and solves the equation for the other.

88. This assumption of a suitable value for one variable and the way in which he selected unknowns of a particular form make the analysis somewhat empirical. An example will illustrate this. He wants to divide a number, such as 13 which is the sum of two squares 4 and 9, into two other squares. He says that since the given squares are 2^2 and 3^2 he will take $(x+2)^2$ and $(mx-3)^2$ as the required squares. He then assumes $m=2$, though any numerical value will do equally well. Hence he has $(x+2)^2 + (2x-3)^2 = 13$. Therefore $x = 8/5$. Hence the required squares are $324/25$ and $1/25$.

89. Diophantus also wrote a third work, entitled *Porisms*. This is now lost, but we have the enunciations of some of the propositions. Among the more striking of these results are the statements that the difference of two cubes can be always expressed as the sum of two cubes;

C

that no number of the form $4n-1$ can be expressed as the sum of two squares; and that no number of the form $8n-1$ (or possibly $24n+7$) can be expressed as the sum of three squares: to these we may perhaps add the proposition that any number can be expressed as a square or as the sum of two or three or four squares.

90. The writings of Diophantus exercised no perceptible influence on Greek mathematics; but his *Arithmetic* attracted the attention of the Arabian school. An imperfect copy of the original work was discovered at Rome in 1462; it was translated into Latin and published by Xylander in 1575; the translation excited general interest, but by that time the European algebraists had on the whole advanced beyond the point at which Diophantus had left off.

91. **The Fifth Century.** Towards the close of the fourth century the growing power of the eastern church enabled it to gratify its hostility to teachers of science. The consequent persecution culminated in the murder of Hypatia at Alexandria in 415. After this many of the Alexandrian students took refuge in Athens, where a small body of teachers had existed from the time of Plato, but these immigrants carried on their work under great difficulties. At last, after several attempts, the Christians got a decree from Justinian in 529 that "heathen learning" should no longer be studied at Athens.

92. The church at Alexandria was less influential, and the city was more remote from the centre of civil power, so that even after the triumphs of the ecclesiastics at the close of the fourth century, the schools there were suffered to continue; but all interest in the study of mathematics had gone, while the endless discussions by the Christians on theological dogmas and the increasing insecurity of the empire tended to divert men's thoughts into other channels.

93. **End of the Second Alexandrian School.** The precarious existence and unfruitful history of the last two centuries of the second Alexandrian school need no record.

In 632 Mohammed died, and within ten years his successors
had subdued Syria, Palestine, Mesopotamia, Persia, and
Egypt.   The precise date on which Alexandria fell is
doubtful, but the most reliable Arab historians give Dec.
10, 641.

94. **Preservation of Alexandrian Works.**   The
works of the more important Alexandrian writers were
preserved in two ways.   In the first place, after the con-
quest of Egypt by the Arabs, some of the philosophers
previously resident there migrated to Constantinople,
which then became the centre of Greek learning in the
East, and remained so until its capture by the Turks in
1453.   The history of this *Byzantine school* has little
scientific interest, but the school preserved the works of
various Alexandrian writers, and in the fifteenth century
the revelation of these works to the West gave a great
stimulus to the study of science (see below, art. 134).

In the second place, the Arabian conquerors gladly
availed themselves of the medical knowledge of the
Greeks; ultimately this led to a series of translations
into Arabic of most of the Greek scientific works then
procurable, including many on mathematical subjects.
These translations circulated as far west as Morocco and
Spain, and thence a knowledge of them passed into
western Europe (see below, arts. 117, 118, 122).

The Mathematics of the Middle Ages.

95. **History of European Mathematics.**   The
mathematics of modern Europe can be traced in un-
broken ascent to the teaching given in the cathedral
schools and monasteries in western Europe.   This was
largely based on the mathematics derived from Roman
sources; and this, in its turn, was founded on the teaching

of the Greeks.   I have discussed Greek mathematics, and on Roman mathematics there is but little to say.

96. **Roman Mathematics.**   At Rome there was no indigenous school of mathematics.   The chief study of the place was the art of government, whether by law, by persuasion, or by those material means on which all government ultimately rests.   Moreover, not only was the genius of the people essentially practical, but, alike during the building of their empire, while it lasted, and under the Goths, the conditions were unfavourable to abstract science.   There were, doubtless, professors who could teach the results of Greek science, but there was no demand for a school of mathematics.   Italians who wished to learn more than the elements of the science went to Alexandria, or to places which drew their inspiration from Alexandria.

97. The subject, as taught in the mathematical schools at Rome, seems to have been generally confined to the practical parts of arithmetic (no doubt, taught by the aid of the abacus), may-be some of the easier properties of numbers, a few practical rules in geometry, and perhaps the elements of Euclid, though some of the arts founded on a knowledge of mathematics were carried to a high pitch of excellence.

98. **Education in the Sixth, Seventh, and Eighth Centuries.**   The early history of medieval mathematics is singularly barren of interest.   Broadly speaking, we may say that from the sixth to the eighth century the only places of study in western Europe were the Benedictine monasteries.   We may find there some slight attempts at a study of literature, but the science usually taught was confined to the use of the abacus, the method of keeping accounts, and a knowledge of the rule by which the date of Easter could be determined.   Nor was this unreasonable, for the monk had renounced the world, and there was no reason why he should learn more

science than was required for the services of the church
and his monastery. The traditions of Greek and Alexandrian learning gradually died away. Possibly in Rome
and a few favoured places, copies of the works of the
great Greek mathematicians were obtainable (though
with difficulty); but there were no students, the books
were unvalued, and gradually became scarce. At the
same time it must be remembered that there was no
active opposition to science, and the western church
did not shew the bitter hostility to it which was so
prominent among the Greek and Asiatic Christians.

99. **Boethius** and **Cassiodorus.** Two authors of the
sixth century—Boethius and Cassiodorus—may be named
whose writings serve as a connecting link between the
mathematics of classical and of medieval times.

Of these the most famous was *Boethius* (475-526), who
was the last Roman of note to study the language and
literature of Greece. His works afforded to medieval
Europe some glimpse of the intellectual life of the old
world, and thus his importance in the history of literature
is great, but it arises merely from the accident of the
time at which he lived. He published a geometry which
contained the enunciations (only) of the first book of
Euclid and of a few selected propositions in the third
and fourth books, together with numerous practical
applications to finding areas, etc.; to it was added an
appendix containing the proofs of the first three propositions to shew that the enunciations might be relied
on. He also wrote an arithmetic.

A few years later *Cassiodorus* discussed the measure of
a liberal education, which, after the preliminary trivium
of grammar, logic, and rhetoric, meant the quadrivium
of arithmetic, geometry, music, and astronomy.

100. **The Cathedral and Conventual Schools.** When
in the latter half of the eighth century Charles the Great
had established his empire, he commanded that schools

should be opened in connection with the cathedrals and monasteries in his kingdom. Probably we shall be correct in saying that such mathematics as were taught at one of these schools did not go beyond the geometry of Boethius, the use of the abacus and multiplication table, and possibly the arithmetic of Boethius; while except there or in a Benedictine cloister it was hardly possible to get opportunities for study. It was of course natural that the works used should come from Roman sources, for western Europe continued to regard Rome as the centre of civilization, and the higher clergy kept up a tolerably constant intercourse with Rome.

101. **Education in the Ninth and Tenth Centuries.** After the death of Charles many of the schools neglected science, confining themselves to teaching Latin, music, and theology. The continued existence of the schools gave, however, an opportunity to any scholar whose learning or zeal exceeded the narrow limits fixed by tradition, and the number of those desiring instruction was so large that a good teacher was tolerably certain to attract a considerable audience, but the science taught still rarely meant more than arithmetic sufficient to enable one to keep accounts, music for the church services, geometry for the purpose of land-surveying, and astronomy sufficient to enable one to calculate the feasts and fasts of the church. The seven liberal arts (trivium and quadrivium) are enumerated in the line, *Lingua, tropus, ratio; numerus, tonus, angulus, astra.* Any student who got beyond the trivium was looked on as a man of great erudition, *Qui tria, qui septem, qui totum scibile novit.* The special questions which then and long afterwards attracted the best thinkers were logic and certain portions of transcendental theology and philosophy. We may sum the matter up by saying that during the ninth and tenth centuries the mathematics taught was usually confined to that comprised in the two works of Boethius together

with the practical use of the abacus and the multiplication table, though during the latter part of the time a wider range of reading was practicable in a few localities.

102. **Gerbert.** In the tenth century learning received a stimulus from the interest taken in it by Gerbert, who became Pope in 999 under the title of Sylvester II. He himself wrote an arithmetic, a geometry, and a tract on the use of the abacus.

103. In the abacus he introduced an improvement by marking each of the nine beads in every column with a distinctive sign, the first bead with a mark denoting 1, the second bead with a mark denoting 2, and so on. These marks, called *apices*, were probably of Indian or Arabic origin, and lead to a representation of numbers essentially the same as the Gobar numerals reproduced below (art. 132) : there was, however, no symbol for zero.

104. **Rise of Medieval Universities.** At the end of the eleventh century, or the beginning of the twelfth, a great revival of learning took place at several of these schools; or perhaps we should rather say that in some cases teachers who were not members of the school settled in its vicinity and with the sanction of the authorities gave lectures, which in fact were always on theology, logic, or civil law. As the students at these centres grew in numbers, it became possible and desirable to act together whenever any interest common to all was concerned. The association thus formed was a sort of guild or trades union. This was the first stage in the history of every medieval university. If successful and likely to be permanent, its members next asked the state for legal privileges, which were almost invariably granted. The last step in the evolution of a medieval university was the acknowledgment of its corporate existence by the pope (or emperor), and the recognition of its degrees as a title to teach throughout Christendom :

thenceforward it became a recognized member of a body of closely connected corporations.

105. **Education at a Medieval University.** At a medieval university the students entered when quite young, sometimes not being more than eleven or twelve years old when first coming into residence. It is misleading to describe them as undergraduates, for their age, their studies, the discipline to which they were subjected, and their position in the university shew that they should be regarded as schoolboys. The first four years of their residence were supposed to be spent in the study of the trivium, *i.e.* Latin grammar, logic, and rhetoric. The majority of students in quite early times did not progress beyond the study of Latin grammar—they formed an inferior faculty and were eligible only for the degree of Master of Grammar—but the more advanced students (and in later times all students) spent these years in the study of the trivium.

The title of Bachelor of Arts was conferred at the end of this course, and signified that the student was no longer a schoolboy. The average age of a commencing bachelor was about seventeen or eighteen. A bachelor could not take pupils, could teach only under special restrictions, and probably occupied a position closely analogous to that of an undergraduate now-a-days. Some few bachelors proceeded to the study of civil or canon law, but it was assumed that the rest studied science and mathematics (the quadrivium) for the next three years; in practice, until the renaissance, most of them devoted this time to logic, philosophy, and theology.

The degree of Master of Arts was given at the end of this course. In the twelfth and thirteenth centuries it was merely a license to teach: no one sought it who did not intend to use it for that purpose and to reside in the university, and only those who had a natural aptitude for such work were likely to enter a profession so ill-paid as that of a teacher. The degree was obtainable by any student who had gone through the recognized course of study and shewn that he was of good moral character. Towards the end of the fourteenth century students began to find that a degree had a pecuniary value, and most universities subsequently conferred it only on condition that the new master should reside and teach for at least a year. A little later the universities took a further step and refused degrees to those who were not intellectually qualified.

106. **Development of Mathematics in India and among the Arabs.** We have now arrived at a time when the results of Arab and Alexandrian science became known in Europe, and I must temporarily leave the subject of medieval mathematics in order to trace the development of the Arabian schools to the same date; I must then explain how the schoolmen became acquainted with the Arab and Greek text-books, and how their introduction affected the progress of European mathematics.

107. In India a school of mathematics of considerable power was developed by the Aryan conquerors. Their geometry was probably derived to a large extent from Greek sources, but their arithmetic, algebra, and perhaps trigonometry were largely their own creation. Among their earliest teachers the names of *Arya-Bhata*, circ. 500, and *Brahmagupta*, circ. 630, are pre-eminent. The school to which these writers belonged introduced the decimal system of numeration; created a rhetorical algebra; applied it to the solution of equations and various problems; and made use of trigonometry as an adjunct to astronomy.

108. The Arabs had always had some commerce with India, and with the establishment of their empire the intercourse naturally increased. The introduction of Indian science into Arabia, and the adoption of the decimal

system of numeration, took place probably towards the close of the eighth century. Many of the scientific works of the Greeks were also easily accessible, and before the end of the ninth century translations of the works of Euclid, Archimedes, Apollonius, Ptolemy, and other Alexandrian writers had been prepared under the authority of the caliphs.

109. **Alkarismi.** The first and in some respects the most illustrious of the Arabian mathematicians was *Mohammed ibn Musa Abu Djefar Al-Khwārizmī*, usually known as *Alkarismi*. About 830 he published an algebra: this treatise holds an important place in the history of mathematics, for the subsequent Arabian and the early medieval works on algebra were largely founded on it. The medieval arithmetic and algebra to which it led was commonly known as algorism. The work is termed *Al-gebr we' l mukabala*: *al-gebr*, from which the word algebra is derived, may be translated by *the restoration*, and refers to the fact that any the same magnitude may be added to or subtracted from both sides of an equation; *al mukabala* means the process of simplification, and is generally used in connection with the combination of like terms into a single term. The unknown quantity is termed either "the thing" or "the root of a plant," and from the latter phrase our use of the word root as applied to the solution of an equation is derived. All the known quantities are numbers, and the algebra is rhetorical.

110. The work is divided into five parts. In the first Alkarismi gave (without proofs) rules for the solution of quadratic equations. He considered only real and positive roots, but he recognized the existence of two roots, which as far as we know was never done by the Greeks. It is somewhat curious that when both roots are positive he generally took only that root which is derived from the negative value of the radical.

He next gave geometrical proofs of these rules in a manner analogous to that of Euclid II. 4. For example, to solve the equation $x^2 + 10x = 39$, or any equation of the form $x^2 + px = q$, he used two methods, of which one is as follows. Let AB represent the value of x, and construct on it the square $ABCD$ (see figure below). Produce DA to H and DC to F so that $AH = CF = 5$ (or $\frac{1}{2}p$); and complete the figure as drawn below. Then the areas AC, HB, and BF represent respectively the magnitudes x^2, $5x$ and $5x$. Thus the left-hand side of the equation is represented by the sum of the areas AC, HB, and BF, that is, by the gnomon HCG. To both sides of the equation add

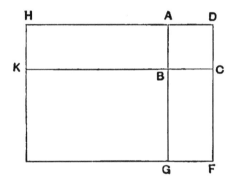

the square KG, the area of which is 25 (or $\frac{1}{4}p^2$), and we shall get a new square whose area is by hypothesis equal to $39 + 25$, that is, to 64 (or $q + \frac{1}{4}p^2$) and whose side therefore is 8. The side of this square DH which is equal to 8 will exceed AH which is equal to 5 by the value of the unknown required, which therefore is 3.

In the third part of the book Alkarismi considered the product of binomials like $x \pm a$ and $x \pm b$. In the fourth part he stated the rules for addition and subtraction of expressions which involve the unknown, its square, or its square root; gave rules for the calculation of square roots; and concluded with the theorems that $a\sqrt{b} = \sqrt{a^2 b}$ and $\sqrt{a}\sqrt{b} = \sqrt{ab}$. In the fifth and last part he solved some problems, such, for example, as to find two numbers whose sum is 10 and the difference of whose squares is 40.

111. Progress of the Arab Schools. After the death of Alkarismi, algebra developed rapidly, but it remained entirely rhetorical. The problems with which the Arabs were concerned were either the solution of equations, problems leading to equations, or properties of numbers. The two most prominent algebraists of a later date were *Alkayami* and *Alkarki*, who flourished at the beginning of the eleventh century. Even where the methods of Arab algebra are general the applications are confined to numerical problems, and the algebra is so arithmetical that it is difficult to treat the subjects apart. From their books on arithmetic and from the observations scattered through various works on algebra we may say that the methods used by the Arabs in arithmetic for multiplication and division were analogous to, though more cumbrous than, those now in use; but the problems to which the subject was applied were similar to those given in modern books, and were solved by similar methods, such as rule of three, etc.

112. I am not concerned with the Arabian views of astronomy or the value of their observations, but I may remark in passing that the Arabs accepted the theory as laid down by Hipparchus and Ptolemy, and did not materially alter or advance it.

113. Like the Greeks, the Arabs used trigonometry only in connection with astronomy; but they introduced the trigonometrical expressions which are now current, and worked out the plane trigonometry of a single angle. They were also acquainted with the elements of spherical trigonometry.

114. In the course of the twelfth century *Bhaskara*, another mathematician of the first rank, appeared in India. His algebra shews a great advance over that of his predecessors, for it is syncopated and almost symbolic. His arithmetic contains a clear statement of the decimal system

of numeration, and the use of the symbol for zero. His geometry is founded on that of Greek writers. This work was known to the Arabs immediately after its publication.

115. From this rapid sketch it will be seen that the work of the Arabs in arithmetic, algebra, and trigonometry was of a high order of excellence. They appreciated geometry and the applications of geometry to astronomy, though they did not extend the bounds of these sciences : but they made no special progress in statics, or optics, or hydrostatics, although there is abundant evidence that they had a thorough knowledge of many branches of practical science.

It is unnecessary to describe further the history of the Arab and Indian schools. They produced no other mathematician of exceptional genius, nor did their subsequent writers materially affect the progress of the science in Europe.

116. **The Introduction of Arabian works into Europe.** In articles 98 to 105 I have discussed the development of European mathematics to a date which corresponds roughly with the end of the "dark ages"; and in articles 106 to 115 I have traced the history of the mathematics of the Hindoos and Arabs to the same date. The mathematics of the two or three centuries that follow are characterized by the introduction into Europe of the Arabian mathematical text-books and of Greek books derived from Arabian sources, and the assimilation of the new ideas thus presented.

117. It was, however, from Spain and not from Arabia that Arabian mathematics came into western Europe. The Moors had established their rule in Spain in 747, and by the tenth or eleventh century had attained a high degree of civilization. Though their political relations with the caliphs at Bagdad were somewhat unfriendly, they gave a ready welcome to the works of the great Arabian mathematicians. In this way the Arab translations of the

writings of Euclid, Archimedes, Apollonius, Ptolemy, and perhaps of other Greek authors, together with the works of the Arabian algebraists, were read and commented on at the three Moorish universities or schools of Granada, Cordova, and Seville.

118. During the eleventh, twelfth, and thirteenth centuries several individual Christian mathematicians got access to these works, and disseminated knowledge of them in Europe. The early years of the thirteenth century are memorable for the development of several universities, and for the appearance of three remarkable mathematicians—Leonardo of Pisa, Jordanus, and Roger Bacon the Franciscan monk of Oxford.

119. **Leonardo.** Leonardo of Pisa was born in 1175; his father was a merchant, who had charge of a custom-house in Barbary; there Leonardo was educated, and became acquainted with the Arabic system of numeration, as also with Alkarismi's work on algebra. Leonardo returned to Italy about 1200, and in 1202 published a work known as the *Liber Abaci*. In it he explained the Arabic system of numeration, and remarked on its advantages over the Roman system. He then gave an account of algebra, and pointed out the convenience of using geometry to get rigid demonstrations of algebraical formulae. He shewed how to solve simple equations, solved a few quadratic equations, and stated some methods for the solution of indeterminate equations; these rules were illustrated by problems on numbers. All the algebra is rhetorical. This work had a wide circulation.

120. The *Liber Abaci* is interesting in the history of arithmetic since it practically introduced the general use of the Arabic numerals into Christian Europe. It is, however, probable that many travellers and the more important merchants were already acquainted with the system as being current in the East. The majority of mathematicians must have also known of it. Leonardo,

however, shewed conclusively the superiority of the Arabic over the Roman system. The use of the Arabic symbols soon extended, and we may consider that by the year 1300, or at the latest 1350, these numerals were familiar to mathematicians and to Italian merchants. I add later some further notes on the history of these symbols.

121. So great was Leonardo's reputation that the emperor Frederick II. stopped at Pisa in 1225 in order to test Leonardo's skill by propounding certain problems. The first question was to find a number of which the square when either increased or decreased by 5 would remain a square: Leonardo gave an answer, which is correct, namely, 41/12. The next question was to find by the methods used in the tenth book of Euclid a line whose length x should satisfy the equation $x^3 + 2x^2 + 10x = 20$: Leonardo shewed by geometry that the problem was impossible, but he gave an approximate value of the root of this equation, namely, $1 \cdot 22'\ 7''\ 42'''\ 33''''\ 4^{\text{v}}\ 40^{\text{vi}}$, which is equal to $1 \cdot 3688081075\ldots$, and is correct to nine places of decimals. Another question was as follows. Three men, A, B, C, possess a sum of money u, their shares being in the ratio $3 : 2 : 1$. A takes away x, keeps half of it, and deposits the remainder with D; B takes away y, keeps two-thirds of it, and deposits the remainder with D; C takes away all that is left, namely z, keeps five-sixths of it, and deposits the remainder with D. This deposit with D is found to belong to A, B, and C in equal proportions. Find u, x, y, and z. Leonardo shewed that the problem was indeterminate and gave as one solution $u = 47$, $x = 33$, $y = 13$, $z = 1$.

122. **Frederick II., 1194-1250.** The emperor Frederick II. did as much as any other single man of the thirteenth century to disseminate a knowledge of the works of the Arab mathematicians in western Europe. The universities of Naples and Padua remain as monuments of his munificence; he having founded the former in 1224, and the latter in 1238. At that time the presence of

Jewish physicians was tolerated in Spain on account of their medical skill and scientific knowledge. Frederick made use of this fact to engage a staff of learned Jews to obtain for him copies of the Arab works and editions of Greek authors in circulation there, and to translate them; by the end of the thirteenth century translations of the works of Euclid, Archimedes, Apollonius, Ptolemy, and of several Arab authors were obtainable from this source. From this time then we may say that the development of science in Europe was independent of the aid of the Arabian schools.

123. **Jordanus.** Among Leonardo's contemporaries was a German mathematician, Jordanus, whose works were almost unknown until the last few years. Of the details of his life we know but little, save that he was elected general of the Dominican order in 1222. His writings on geometry shew great learning; but those on arithmetic and algebra are especially remarkable. In them letters are employed to denote both known and unknown quantities, and are used in the demonstrations of the rules of arithmetic as well as of algebra. As an example of this I quote his solution of the problem to determine two quantities whose sum and product are known. His argument is as follows. Let the numbers be $a + b$ (which I will denote by γ) and c. Then $\gamma + c$ is given; hence $(\gamma + c)^2$ is known; denote it by e. Again γc is given; denote it by d; hence $4\gamma c$, which is equal to $4d$, is known; denote it by f. Then $(\gamma - c)^2$ is equal to $e - f$, which is known; denote it by g. Therefore $\gamma - c = \sqrt{g}$, which is known; denote it by h. Hence $\gamma + c$ and $\gamma - c$ are known, and therefore γ and c can be at once found. It is curious that he should have taken a sum like $a + b$ for one of his unknowns. In a numerical illustration he takes the sum to be 10 and the product 21.

124. The above is the earliest instance known in European mathematics of syncopated algebra, in which letters

are used for algebraical symbols. It is, however, doubtful how far the works of Jordanus materially influenced the development of algebra. In fact, in the history of mathematics, improvements in notation or method were often made long before they were generally adopted or their advantages realized, and it was not until the general standard of knowledge almost necessitated such an improvement, or it was enforced by some one whose zeal or attainments· compelled attention, that it came into general use.

125. It is not necessary to describe in detail the mechanics, optics, or astronomy of Jordanus. The treatment of mechanics throughout the middle ages was generally unintelligent.

126. No mathematicians of the same ability as Leonardo and Jordanus appear in the history of the subject for over two hundred years. Their individual achievements must not be taken to imply the standard of knowledge then current, but their works were accessible to students in the following two centuries, though there were not many who seem to have derived much benefit therefrom.

127. **Roger Bacon, 1214-1294.** A contemporary of Leonardo and Jordanus, who, for physical science, did work somewhat analogous to what they did for arithmetic and algebra, was Roger Bacon. He was educated at Oxford and Paris, and spent some years in the former city, occupied in teaching science. He stated as a fundamental principle that its study must rest solely on experiment. He strove to replace logic in the university curriculum by mathematical and linguistic studies, but the influences of the age were too strong for him, and his glowing eulogy on " divine mathematics," which should form the foundation of a liberal education and which "alone can purge the intellect and fit the student for the acquirement of all knowledge," fell on deaf ears. We can judge how small was the amount of geometry

D

which was implied in the quadrivium when he tells us
that in geometry few students at Oxford in his day read
beyond Euc. I. 5.

128. **The Fourteenth Century.** The history of the
fourteenth century, like that of the one preceding it, is
mostly concerned with the introduction and assimilation
of Arabian mathematical text-books and of Greek books
derived from Arabian sources. By the middle of this
century Euclidean geometry and algorism were fairly
familiar to all professed mathematicians, and the Ptolemaic
astronomy was also generally known. About this time
the almanacks began to add to the explanation of the
Arabic symbols the rules of addition, subtraction, multiplication, and division, " de algorismo." The more
important calendars and other treatises also inserted a
statement of the rules of proportion, illustrated by various
practical questions.

129. In the latter half of this century there was a
revolt of the universities against the intellectual tyranny
of the schoolmen. The result of these influences on the
study of mathematics may be seen in the changes then
introduced in the study of the quadrivium. Thus at
Prague, in 1384, candidates for the bachelor's degree
were required to have read a specified treatise on the
sphere, and candidates for the master's degree to be
acquainted with the first six books of Euclid, optics,
hydrostatics, the theory of the lever, and astronomy.
Lectures were actually delivered on arithmetic, the art of
reckoning with the fingers, and the algorism of integers;
on almanacks, which probably meant elementary astrology; and on Ptolemaic astronomy. Similarly at Vienna,
in 1389, a candidate for a master's degree was required
to have read five books of Euclid, common perspective,
proportional parts, the measurement of superficies, and a
treatise on the theory of the planets founded on Ptolemy's
work. This was a fairly respectable mathematical standard

but I would remind the reader that there was no such thing as "plucking" in a medieval university. The student had to keep an act or give a lecture on certain subjects, but whether he did it well or badly he got his degree, and it is probable that it was only the few students whose interests were mathematical who really mastered the subjects mentioned above.

130. **The Fifteenth Century.** A few facts gleaned from the history of the fifteenth century tend to shew that the regulations about the study of the quadrivium were not seriously enforced. The lecture lists for the years 1437 and 1438 of the university of Leipzig (the statutes of which are almost identical with those of Prague) are extant, and shew that the only lectures given there on mathematics in those years were confined to astrology. The records of Bologna, Padua, and Pisa seem to imply that there also astrology was the sole scientific subject taught in the fifteenth century. The only mathematical subjects mentioned in the registers of the university of Oxford as read there between the years 1449 and 1463 were Ptolemy's astronomy (or some commentary on it) and the first two books of Euclid. Whether most students got as far as this is doubtful. It would seem, from an edition of Euclid's *Elements* published at Paris in 1536, that after 1452 candidates for the master's degree at that university had to take an oath that they had attended lectures on the first six books of that work.

131. By the middle of the fifteenth century printing was invented, and the facilities it gave for disseminating knowledge were so great as to revolutionize the progress of science, and perhaps this is as good a date as can be fixed for the end of the middle ages.

132. **The Arabic Numerals.** As I have alluded frequently to the Arabic system of numerical notation, I may add a few notes on the history of the symbols now current.

Their origin is obscure. On the whole it seems probable that the symbols for the numbers 4, 5, 6, 7, and 9 (and possibly 8 too) are derived from the initial letters of the corresponding words in the Indo-Bactrian alphabet in use in the north of India perhaps 150 years. before Christ; that the symbols for the numbers 2 and 3 are derived respectively from two and three parallel penstrokes written cursively; and, similarly, that the symbol

Devanagari (Indian) numerals, *circ.* 950.

Gobar Arabic numerals, *circ.* 1100 (?)

From a missal, *circ.* 1385, of German origin.

European (probably Italian) numerals, *circ.* 1400.

From the *Mirrour of the World*, printed by Caxton in 1480.

From a Scotch calendar for 1482, probably of French origin.

for the number 1 represents a single penstroke. Numerals of this type were in use in India before the end of the second century of our era. The origin of the symbol for zero is uncertain, but it is possible that it was originally a dot inserted to indicate a blank space; there is reason to believe that it was introduced in India towards the close of the fifth century of our era, though the earliest writing now extant in which it occurs is assigned to the eighth century.

The numerals used in India, in and after the eighth

century, are termed Devanagari numerals, and their forms
are shewn in the first line of the table given on the
opposite page. The symbols finally used by the Arabs are
termed Gobar numerals, and an idea of the forms most
commonly employed may be gathered from those printed
in the second line of the table given above. From Spain
or Barbary the Gobar numerals passed into western
Europe. The further evolution of the forms of the
symbols to those with which we are familiar is indicated
above by facsimiles of the numerals used at different
times. All the sets of numerals here represented are
written from left to right and in the order 1, 2, 3, 4, 5,
6, 7, 8, 9, 10. From 1500 onwards the symbols employed
are practically the same as those now in use.

133. **Introduction of the Arabic numerals into
common use.** Leaving now the history of the symbols,
I proceed to discuss their introduction into general use.
I have already explained how men of science and
astronomers had become acquainted with the Arabic
system by the middle of the thirteenth century. The
trade of Europe during the thirteenth and fourteenth
centuries was mostly in Italian hands, and the obvious
advantages of the algoristic system led to its general
adoption in Italy for mercantile purposes. This change
was not effected, however, without considerable opposition ;
thus an edict was issued at Florence in 1299 forbidding
bankers to use Arabic numerals, and the authorities of
the university of Padua in 1348 directed that a list should
be kept of books for sale with the prices marked "non
per cifras sed per literas claras."

The rapid spread of the use of Arabic numerals and
arithmetic through the rest of Europe seems to have
been as largely due to the makers of almanacks and
calendars as to merchants and men of science. These
calendars had a wide circulation. They were of two
types. Some of them were composed with special refer-

ence to ecclesiastical purposes, and contained the dates of the different festivals and fasts of the church for a period of some seven or eight years in advance, as well as notes on church ritual. Nearly every monastery and church of any pretensions possessed one of these, and numerous specimens are still extant. Those of the second type were written specially for the use of astrologers and physicians, and the better specimens contained notes on various scientific subjects (especially medicine and astronomy); these were not then uncommon, but since it was only rarely that they found their way into any corporate library, specimens are now scarce. The Arabic symbols were generally employed in both kinds of almanacks, and there are few, if any, specimens of calendars issued after the year 1300 in which an explanation of their use is not included. Towards the middle of the fourteenth century the rules of arithmetic *de algorismo* were also added, and by the year 1400 we may consider that the Arabic symbols were generally known throughout Europe, and were commonly used in scientific and astronomical works.

Outside Italy most merchants continued, however, to keep their accounts in Roman numerals till about 1550, and monasteries and colleges till about 1650; though in both cases it is probable that in and after the fifteenth century the processes of arithmetic were performed in the algoristic manner. No instance of a date or number being written in Arabic numerals is known to occur in any English parish register or the court rolls of any English manor before the sixteenth century; but in the rent roll of the St. Andrews Chapter, Scotland, the Arabic numerals are used in an entry in the year 1490. The Arabic numerals were introduced into Constantinople at about the same time as into Italy.

The Mathematics of the Renaissance.

134. Commencement of the Renaissance. Mathematicians had barely assimilated the knowledge obtained from the Arabs, including their translations of the works of Greek writers, when the refugees who escaped from Constantinople after the fall of the eastern empire brought with them the original books and the traditions of Greek science. Thus by the middle of the fifteenth century the chief results of Greek and Arabian mathematics were accessible to European students. The invention of printing about this time rendered the dissemination of discoveries comparatively easy, and this revolutionized the progress of science.

The introduction of printing marks the beginning of the modern world, and was contemporaneous with an outburst of activity in all branches of learning. The creation of a fresh group of universities (including those in Scotland) of a somewhat less complex type than the medieval universities testify to the general desire for knowledge. The discovery of America in 1492, and the discussions that preceded the Reformation flooded Europe with new ideas which by the invention of printing were widely disseminated; and the advance in mathematics was as pronounced as that in literature, art, and politics.

135. Regiomontanus, 1436-1476. Amongst the earliest writers of this period was Regiomontanus. He studied mathematics under Purbach at the university of Vienna; then, after spending some ten years in travel, he settled (in 1471) for a few years at Nuremberg, where he established an observatory, opened a printing-press, and probably lectured. Thence he moved to Rome, on an invitation from Sixtus IV., who wished him to reform the calendar. He was assassinated, shortly after his arrival, at the age of forty.

136. Regiomontanus was among the first to take advantage of the recovery of the original texts of the Greek mathematical works. The fruit of this study was shewn in his *De Triangulis* written in 1464. This contains the earliest systematic exposition of trigonometry, plane and spherical, though the only trigonometrical functions introduced are those of the sine and cosine. Algebra is used in it. His trigonometry, like his algebra, is rhetorical, *i.e.* every step of the argument is expressed in words at full length.

137. **Introduction of signs +, −, and =.** About this time some improvements in algebraic notation were introduced, notably the introduction of the current symbols for addition, subtraction, and equality.

One of the earliest instances of the use of the signs + and − occurs in Widman's arithmetic, published in 1489. It has been conjectured that originally these were warehouse marks, but some recent evidence has strengthened a view formerly held that the symbol for *plus* is derived from the Latin abbreviation *&* for *et*; while that for *minus* is obtained from the bar which is often written over the contracted form of a word to signify that certain letters have been left out. These symbols seem to have had their origin in Germany; we find them in ordinary use in England in 1540.

The symbol = for equality was introduced by Record in his *Whetstone of Witte*, London, 1557. He said that this sign was selected because than two parallel straight lines "noe 2 thynges can be moare equalle." It has, however, been remarked that it is a not uncommon abbreviation for the word *est* in medieval manuscripts, and this would seem to indicate a more probable origin.

The introduction of these signs was a mere matter of convenience; they were regarded only as unimportant abbreviations and not as symbols of operation; and no one suspected that their introduction was preparing the way for a revolution of algebraic methods.

138. **Pacioli, circ. 1500.** Lucas Pacioli was born in Tuscany about the middle of the fifteenth century. We know little of his life except that he was a Franciscan friar; and that, after lecturing in various Italian cities, he was appointed the first occupant of a chair of mathematics at Milan; he died at Florence about the year 1510.

139. His chief work, printed at Venice in 1494, consists of two parts, the first dealing with arithmetic and algebra, the second with geometry. This was the earliest printed book on arithmetic and algebra, and its importance is largely due to this and its consequent wide circulation.

140. In the arithmetic Pacioli gave rules for the four simple processes, and a method for extracting square roots. He dealt pretty fully with all questions connected with mercantile arithmetic, in which he worked out numerous examples, and in particular discussed at length bills of exchange and the theory of book-keeping by double entry. This was the earliest publication of a systematic exposition of algoristic arithmetic. Most of the problems are solved by the method of false assumption (see above, art. 79), but there are several numerical mistakes.

141. In the algebra Pacioli found expressions for the sum of the squares and the sum of the cubes of the first n natural numbers. The larger part of this part of the book is taken up with simple and quadratic numerical equations, and problems on numbers which lead to such equations. He mentioned the Arabic classification of cubic equations, but added that their solution appears to be as impossible as the quadrature of the circle. The following is his rule for solving a quadratic equation of the form $x^2 + x = a$: it is rhetorical and not syncopated, and will serve to illustrate the inconvenience of that method. "Si res et census numero coaequantur, a rebus

dimidio sumpto censum producere debes, addereque numero, cujus a radice totiens tolle semis rerum, census latusque redibit." He confined his attention to the positive roots of equations.

142. Much of the matter described above is taken from Leonardo's *Liber Abaci*, but it is expressed in a better notation. Pacioli followed the Arabs in calling the unknown quantity the *thing*, in Italian *cosa*, or in Latin *res*, and sometimes denotes it by *co* or *R* or *Rj*. He called the square of it *census* or *zensus*, and sometimes denoted it by *ce* or *Z*; similarly the cube of it, or *cuba*, is sometimes represented by *cu* or *C*; the fourth power, or *censo di censo*, is written at length, or as *ce di ce*, or as *ce ce*. Addition and equality are indicated by the initial letters of the words *plus* and *aequalis*, but the introduction of a symbol for *minus* is usually evaded by writing the quantities on that side of the equation which makes them positive, though in a few places he denoted it by $\overline{m}$ for *minus* or by *de* for *demptus*. Similar symbols for plus and minus were used by Chuquet of Paris in 1484. The introduction of these contractions, is a commencement of syncopated algebra.

143. There is nothing striking in the results given by Pacioli in the second or geometrical part of his work, nor in other tracts on geometry which he wrote. It may be noticed, however, that, like Regiomontanus, he applied algebra to aid him in investigating the geometrical properties of figures.

144. By the beginning of the sixteenth century the printing press began to be active and many of the works of the earlier mathematicians became now for the first time accessible to all students. This stimulated inquiry, and before the middle of the century numerous works were issued which, though they did not include any great discoveries, introduced a variety of small improvements, all tending to make algebra more analytical, and

to familiarize the public with symbols of abbreviation, if not of operation.

145. **Tartaglia, 1500-1557.** Nicholas Tartaglia, that is, Nicholas the stammerer, was born at Brescia. When he was twelve years old the French captured the town, and in a general massacre which followed their entry, Tartaglia's skull, jaw, and palate were cut open, and he was left for dead. His mother, finding him still alive, managed to carry him off :- deprived of all resources she recollected that dogs when wounded always licked the injured place, and to that remedy he attributed his ultimate recovery, but the injury to his palate produced an impediment in his speech from which he received his nickname. His mother obtained sufficient money to pay for his attendance at school for fifteen days, and he took advantage of it to steal a copy-book from which he subsequently taught himself how to read and write; but so poor were they that he tells us he could not afford to buy paper, and was obliged to make use of the tombstones as slates on which to work his exercises. He commenced his public life by lecturing at Verona, but subsequently was appointed to a chair of mathematics at Venice, which he occupied till his death.

146. In 1535 he became famous through his acceptance of a challenge from a certain *Antonio del Fiori*, who had obtained an empirical solution of a cubic equation of the form $x^3 + qx = r$. Tartaglia had stated that he could effect the solution of a numerical equation of the form $x^3 + px^2 = r$, and Fiori, believing that Tartaglia was an impostor, challenged him to a contest. According to this challenge, each of them was to deposit a stake with a notary, and whoever could solve the most problems out of a collection of thirty propounded by the other was to get the stakes, thirty days being allowed for the solution of the questions proposed. Tartaglia accepted the challenge, and suspecting that the questions proposed

to him would depend on cubic equations he set to work on
their theory, and discovered how to obtain a solution at
any rate in certain cases. His solution is believed to have
depended on a geometrical construction (see below, art.
152). When the contest took place, Tartaglia succeeded
within two hours in bringing all the questions proposed to
him to particular cases of the equation $x^3 + qx = r$, of which
he knew the solution. His opponent failed to solve any of
the problems proposed to him, which as a matter of fact
were all reducible to numerical equations of the form
$x^3 + px^2 = r$.

147. The chief works of Tartaglia are an arithmetic published in 1556, and a treatise on numbers, published in
1560. These works are verbose, but give a clear account
of the different arithmetical methods then in use, and have
numerous historical notes. The former contains an immense
number of questions on every kind of problem which would
be likely to occur in mercantile arithmetic, and there are
several attempts to frame algebraical formulae suitable for
particular problems. In the latter he shewed how the
coefficients of x in expansion of $(1 + x)^n$ could be calculated
from those in the expansion of $(1 + x)^{n-1}$ for the cases when
n is equal to 2, 3, 4, 5, or 6.

148. **Cardan, 1501-1576.** The life of Tartaglia was embittered by a quarrel with his contemporary Cardan, who,
having under a pledge of secrecy obtained Tartaglia's
solution of a cubic equation, published it. Cardan's career
is an account of the most extraordinary and inconsistent
acts. A gambler, if not a murderer, he was also the ardent
student of science, solving problems which had long baffled
investigation ; at one time of his life he was devoted to
intrigues which were a scandal even in Italy in the sixteenth century, at another he raved on astrology, and yet
at another he declared that philosophy was the only subject
worthy of man's attention. His was the genius that was
closely allied to madness.

149. The chief mathematical work of Cardan is the *Ars Magna*, published in 1545. Cardan was much interested in the contest between Tartaglia and Fiori, and as he had already begun writing this book he asked the former to communicate his method of solving a cubic equation. Tartaglia refused. Shortly afterwards Cardan wrote begging Tartaglia to come to Milan to meet an Italian nobleman who was anxious to make his acquaintance: Tartaglia came, and though he found no nobleman awaiting him at the end of his journey, he yielded to Cardan's importunity and gave him the rule he wanted, Cardan on his side taking a solemn oath that he would never reveal it, and would not even commit it to writing in such a way that after his death any one could understand it. He seems, however, to have at once taught the method; and the result was published in 1545.

150. The *Ars Magna* is superior to any algebra previously published. Hitherto algebraists had confined their attention to those roots of equations which were positive. Cardan discussed negative and even imaginary roots, and proved that the latter would always occur in pairs, though he declined to commit himself to any explanation as to the meaning of these " sophistic " quantities which he said were ingenious though useless. Most of his analysis of cubic equations seems to have been original; he shewed that if the three roots were real, Tartaglia's solution gave them in a form which involved imaginary quantities. Except for the somewhat similar researches of Bombelli a few years later, the theory of imaginary quantities received little further attention from mathematicians until Euler took the matter up after the lapse of nearly two centuries. Gauss put the subject on a systematic basis, and introduced the modern notation of complex variables.

151. Cardan established the relations connecting the roots with the coefficients of an equation. He was aware

of the principle that underlies Descartes's "rule of signs," but, since he followed the then general custom of writing his equations as the equality of two expressions in each of which all the terms were positive, he was unable to express the rule concisely. He gave a method of approximating to the root of a numerical equation, founded on the fact that, if a function have opposite signs when two numbers are substituted in it, the equation obtained by equating the function to zero will have a root between those numbers.

152. Cardan's solution of a quadratic equation is geometrical and substantially the same as that given by Alkarismi (see above, art. 110). His solution of a cubic equation is also geometrical. Thus to solve the equation $x^3 + 6x = 20$ (or any equation of the form $x^3 + qx = r$), he found two cubes such that the rectangle under their respective edges is 2 (or $\frac{1}{3}q$) and the difference of their volumes is 20 (or r); and shewed that x will be equal to the difference between the edges of these cubes. To obtain the lengths of the edges of the two cubes he had to solve a quadratic equation for which the geometrical solution previously given sufficed. Like his predecessors, he gave separate proofs of his rule for the different forms of equations which fall under it: thus he proved the rule independently for equations of the form $x^3 + px = q$, $x^3 = px + q$, $x^3 + px + q = 0$, and $x^3 + q = px$. The equations he considered are numerical, but in some of his analysis he used literal coefficients. His pupil Ferrari reduced the solution of a biquadratic to that of a cubic equation: the solution is given in the *Ars Magna* (see below, art. 162).

153. Shortly after Cardan came a number of somewhat mediocre mathematicians, who, however, did good work in disseminating a knowledge of algebra and in investigating plane trigonometrical formulae which involve more than one angle—*ex. gr.* the usual formulae for $\sin(A \pm B)$. About this time, also, several text-books on algebra were

produced : in particular I may mention one by Bombelli, published in 1572.

154. Bombelli's algebra contains a systematic exposition of the knowledge then current. In it he discussed radicals, real and imaginary ; he also treated the theory of equations, and shewed that in the irreducible case of a cubic equation the roots are all real. This work is noticeable for the introduction of an improvement in the notation of algebra. The symbols then ordinarily used for the unknown quantity and its powers were letters which stood for abbreviations of the words. Those most frequently adopted were R or Rj for *radix* or *res* (x), Z or C for *zensus* or *census* (x^2), C or K for *cubus* (x^3), etc. Thus $x^2 + 5x - 4$ would have been written 1 Z p. 5 R m. 4, where p stands for plus and m for minus. Other letters and symbols were also used, and some mathematicians would have written the above expression as $1Q + 5N - 4$. The advance made by Bombelli was that he introduced a symbol ⨆ for the unknown quantity, ⨆ for its square, ⨆ for its cube, and so on, and therefore wrote $x^2 + 5x - 4$ as 1 ⨆ p. 5 ⨆ m. 4. Stevinus in 1586 employed ①, ②, ③, ..., in a similar way. He would have written the above expression as $1② + 5① - 4⓪$. But whether the symbols were more or less convenient they were still only abbreviations for words, and were subject to all the rules of syntax. They merely afforded a sort of shorthand by which the various steps and results could be expressed concisely. The next advance was the creation of symbolic algebra, and the chief credit of that is due to Vieta.

155. **Vieta, 1540-1603.** Vieta was born near la Rochelle : he was brought up as a lawyer, and for some time practised at the Parisian bar, but about 1580 he entered the public service, and after that gave up most of his leisure to mathematics. His reputation was already considerable. When one day the ambassador from the Low Countries remarked to Henry IV. that France did not

possess any geometricians capable of solving a problem
which had been propounded in 1593 by his countryman
Adrian Romanus to all the mathematicians of the world,
and which required the solution of an equation of the
45th degree, Vieta, who was informed of the challenge,
and who was acquainted with the expansion of $\sin n\theta$
in terms of $\sin \theta$ and $\cos \theta$, at once saw that the equation
was satisfied by the chord of a circle (of unit radius) which
subtends an angle $2\pi/45$ at the centre, and in a few minutes
he wrote out a solution of the problem. This achievement
gave him an immense reputation.

156. Vieta issued numerous works on algebra and geometry. The most important was the *In Artem Analyticam
Isagoge*, 1591. This is the earliest work on symbolic
algebra. In it he systematically employed the signs + and
−, and used them as symbols of operation; but he had no
sign to denote equality. He also used letters for both
known and unknown quantities, a notation for the powers
of quantities, and emphasized the advantage of working
with homogeneous equations. To this was added an
appendix on the addition and multiplication of algebraical
quantities, and on the powers of a binomial up to the sixth.
Vieta implied that he knew how to form the coefficients of
these six expansions by means of the arithmetical triangle
as Tartaglia had previously done, but Pascal was the first
to give the general rule for forming it for any order, and
Newton was the first to give the general expression for the
coefficient of x^p in the expansion of $(1+x)^n$. Another
appendix on the solution of equations was subsequently
added.

157. The *In Artem* is memorable for bringing into
general notice two improvements in algebraic notation. In
both Vieta had been forestalled, but it was his good luck
in emphasizing their importance to be the means of making
them generally known at a time when opinion was ripe for
such an advance.

158. One of these improvements was that he denoted the known quantities by the consonants B, C, D, etc., and the unknown quantities by the vowels A, E, I, etc.; thus in any problem a number of unknown quantities could be employed. The present custom of using letters at the beginning of the alphabet a, b, c, etc., to represent known quantities, and those towards the end, x, y, z, etc., to represent the unknown quantities was introduced by Descartes in 1637.

159. The other improvement was this. Till this time it had been the custom to introduce new symbols to represent the square, cube, etc., of quantities which had already occurred in the equations; thus, if R or N stood for x, Z or C or Q stood for x^2, and C or K for x^3, etc. So long as this was the case the chief advantage of algebra was that it afforded a concise statement of results, every statement of which was reasoned out. But when Vieta used A to denote the unknown quantity x, he sometimes employed A *quadratus*, A *cubus*, ..., to represent x^2, x^3,..., which at once shewed the connection between the different powers; and later the successive powers of A were commonly denoted by the abbreviations Aq, Ac, Aqq, etc.

160. In other works Vieta shewed that the first member of an algebraical equation $\phi(x) = 0$ could be resolved into linear factors, and explained how the coefficients of x could be expressed as functions of the roots. He also indicated how from a given equation another could be obtained whose roots were equal to those of the original increased by a given quantity or multiplied by a given quantity; and he used this method to get rid of the coefficient of x in a quadratic equation, and of the coefficient of x^2 in a cubic equation, and was thus enabled to give the general algebraic solution of both.

161. His solution of a cubic equation is as follows. First reduce the equation to the form $x^3 + 3a^2x = 2b^3$. Next let $x = a^2/y - y$, and we get $y^6 + 2b^3y^3 = a^6$, which is a quadratic

E

in y^3. Hence y can be found, and therefore x can be determined.

162. His solution of a biquadratic is similar to Ferrari's, and essentially as follows. He first got rid of the term involving x^3, thus reducing the equation to the form $x^4 + a^2x^2 + b^3x = c^4$. Next he took the terms involving x^2 and x to the right-hand side of the equation and added $x^2y^2 + \frac{1}{4}y^4$ to each side, so that the equation became $(x^2 + \frac{1}{2}y^2)^2 = x^2(y^2 - a^2) - b^3x + \frac{1}{4}y^4 + c^4$. He then chose y, so that the right-hand side of this equality is a perfect square. Substituting this value of y, he was able to take the square root of both sides, and thus obtain two quadratic equations for x, each of which can be solved.

163. **Girard, 1590-1633.** Vieta's results in trigonometry and the theory of equations were extended by Girard, a Dutch mathematician. Girard's chief discoveries are contained in his *Invention nouvelle en l'algèbre*, published in 1629: this contains the earliest use of brackets; a geometrical interpretation of the negative sign; the statement that the number of roots of an algebraical equation is equal to its degree; the distinct recognition of imaginary roots; and probably implies also a knowledge that the first member of an algebraical equation $\phi(x) = 0$ could be resolved into linear factors.

164. **Napier, 1550-1617.** John Napier, the inventor of logarithms, was born at Merchistoun. He spent most of his time on the family estate near Edinburgh, and took an active part in the political and religious controversies of the day. The business of his life was to shew that the pope was anti-Christ, but his favourite amusement was the study of mathematics and science. Besides his invention of logarithms, he introduced in 1617 his "rods," an instrument by the use of which one number can be multiplied or divided by another. Also in spherical trigonometry he discovered certain formulae now known as Napier's analogies, and enunciated a "rule of circular

parts" for the solution of right-angled spherical triangles.

165. **Invention of Logarithms.** As soon as the use
of exponents became common in algebra the invention of
logarithms would naturally follow, but Napier reasoned
out the result without the use of any symbolic notation
to assist him, and the invention was the result of the
efforts of many years to abbreviate the processes of multiplication and division. The discovery was announced in
1614.

166. **Briggs, 1556-1631.** Briggs was educated at Cambridge, and in 1619 became the first occupant of the then
newly founded Savilian chair of geometry at Oxford, a
professorship which he held until his death. It may be
interesting to add that he began his lectures at Oxford
with the ninth proposition of the first book of Euclid,
that being the farthest point to which Savile had been
able to carry his audiences.

167. The almost immediate adoption throughout Europe
of logarithms for astronomical and other calculations was
mainly the work of Briggs, who in 1617 constructed and
issued the first table of common logarithms. Amongst
others he convinced Kepler of the advantages of Napier's
discovery, and the spread of the use of logarithms was
rendered more rapid by the zeal and reputation of Kepler,
who, by his tables of 1625 and 1629, brought them into
vogue in Germany, while Cavalieri in 1624 and Edmund
Wingate in 1626 did a similar service for Italian and
French mathematicians.

168. The introduction in arithmetical processes of the
decimal notation for fractions is also (in my opinion) due
to Briggs. Before the sixteenth century, fractions were
commonly written in the sexagesimal notation (*ex. gr.* see
above, art. 121). Stevinus in 1585 used a decimal notation,
for he wrote a number such as 25·379 either in the form
25, 3′ 7″ 9‴, or in the form 25 ⓪ 3 ① 7 ② 9 ③ ; and

Napier in 1617, in his essay on rods, had adopted the former notation; but these writers employed the notation only as a concise way of stating results, and made no use of it as an operative form. Briggs underlined the decimal figures, and would have printed a number such as 25·379 in the form 25379. Subsequent writers added another line, and would have written it as 25⌊379. It was not till the beginning of the eighteenth century that the notation now current was generally employed.

169. **Harriot, 1560-1620.** Harriot did a great deal to extend and codify the theory of equations. The early part of his life was spent in America with Sir Walter Raleigh. While there he made the first survey of Virginia and North Carolina, the maps of these being subsequently presented to Queen Elizabeth. On his return to England he settled in London, and gave up most of his time to mathematical studies. His *Artis Analyticae Praxis*, first printed in 1631, does not differ essentially from a modern text-book on algebra and the theory of equations; it is more analytical than any algebra that preceded it, and marks a great advance in symbolism and notation. Harriot was, I believe, the earliest writer who realized the advantage to be obtained by taking all the terms of an equation to one side of it. He was the first to use the signs $>$ and $<$ to represent greater than and less than. When he denoted the unknown quantity by a he represented a^2 by aa, a^3 by aaa, and so on. This is a distinct improvement on Vieta's notation. The same symbolism was used as late as 1685, but concurrently with the modern index notation which was introduced by Descartes.

170. **Oughtred, 1576-1660.** Among those who contributed to the general adoption of these additions to algorism and algebra was Oughtred of Cambridge. His *Clavis Mathematicae*, published in 1631, is a systematic text-book on arithmetic. In this work he introduced

the symbol × for multiplication, and the symbol :: in proportion. Previously to his time a proportion such as $a : b = c : d$ was usually written as $a - b - c - d$, but he denoted it by $a . b :: c . d$. Oughtred also wrote a treatise on trigonometry, published in 1657, in which abbreviations for *sine, cosine*, etc., were employed.

171. **The Development of Mechanics.** The closing years of the renaissance were marked by a revival of interest in nearly all branches of mathematics and science. As far as pure mathematics is concerned, we have already seen that during the last half of the sixteenth century there had been a great advance in algebra, theory of equations, and trigonometry, and we shall shortly see that in the early part of the seventeenth century some new processes in geometry were invented. If, however, we turn to applied mathematics, it is impossible not to be struck by the fact that even as late as the middle or end of the sixteenth century the theories of statics (of solids) and hydrostatics remained much as Archimedes had left them, while dynamics as a science did not exist. It was Stevinus who gave the first impulse to the renewed study of statics, and Galileo who laid the foundation of dynamics.

172. **Stevinus.** We know little of the life of Stevinus, save that he was originally a merchant's clerk at Antwerp, and at a later period of his life was the friend of Prince Maurice of Orange, by whom he was made quarter-master-general of the Dutch army.

I have already alluded to his introduction of exponents to mark the power to which quantities were raised; for instance, he wrote $3x^2 - 5x + 1$ as $3 ② - 5 ① + 1 ⓪$. His notation for decimal fractions was of a similar character. He likewise suggested a decimal system of weights and measures.

173. It is, however, on his *Statics and Hydrostatics*, published (in Flemish) in 1586, that his reputation rests.

In this work he enunciated the triangle of forces—a theorem which some think was first propounded by Leonardo da Vinci. Stevinus regarded this as the fundamental proposition of the subject. Previous to the publication of his work, the science of statics had rested on the theory of the lever, but subsequently it became usual to commence by proving the possibility of representing forces by straight lines, and so of reducing many theorems to geometrical propositions, and in particular to obtaining in that way a proof of the parallelogram or triangle of forces. Stevinus's exposition was obscure, and the new treatment of the subject was not definitely established before the appearance, in 1687, of Varignon's work on mechanics. Stevinus also found the force which must be exerted along the line of greatest slope to support a given weight on an inclined plane—a problem the solution of which had been in dispute. He further distinguished between stable and unstable equilibrium. In hydrostatics he discussed the question of the pressure which a fluid can exercise, and explained the so-called hydrostatic paradox.

174. **Galileo, 1564-1642.** Just as the modern treatment of statics originates with Stevinus, so the foundation of the science of dynamics is due to Galileo. Galileo, a descendant of an old and noble Florentine house, was sent at the age of seventeen to the university of Pisa to study medicine. It was there that he noticed that the great bronze lamp, which still hangs from the roof of the cathedral, performed its oscillations in equal times independently of the extent of the oscillations. He had been hitherto purposely kept in ignorance of mathematics, but one day, by chance hearing a lecture on geometry, he was so fascinated by the science that he thenceforward devoted all his leisure to its study, and finally he got leave to discontinue his medical studies. He left the university in 1586, and almost immediately commenced his original researches.

175. He published in 1587 an account of the hydrostatic balance, and in 1588 an essay on the centre of gravity in solids. The fame of these works secured for him the appointment to the mathematical chair at Pisa. During the next three years he carried on from the leaning tower a series of experiments on falling bodies which established the first principles of dynamics. In 1592 he was appointed professor at Padua, a chair which he held for eighteen years. His lectures there seem to have been chiefly on mechanics and hydrostatics, and the substance of them is contained in his treatise on mechanics which was published in 1612.

176. In these lectures he demonstrated that falling bodies did not (as was then believed) descend with velocities proportional amongst other things to their weights. He further shewed that, if it were assumed that they descended with a uniformly accelerated motion, it was possible to deduce the relations connecting velocity, space, and time which did actually exist. At a later date, by observing the times of descent of bodies sliding down inclined planes, he shewed that this hypothesis was true. He also proved that the path of a projectile was a parabola. The laws of motion are, however, nowhere enunciated definitely, and Galileo must be regarded rather as preparing the way for Newton than as being himself the creator of the science of dynamics. In statics he laid down the principle that in machines what was gained in power was lost in speed, and in the same ratio. In the statics of solids he found the force which can support a given weight on an inclined plane; in hydrostatics he propounded the more elementary theorems on pressure and on floating bodies; while among hydrostatical instruments he used, and perhaps invented, the thermometer, though in a somewhat imperfect form.

177. The details of Galileo's astronomical researches lie outside the range of this book, but it may be interesting

to give the leading facts. In 1609 Galileo heard that a tube containing lenses had been made in Holland which served to magnify objects seen through it. This gave him the clue, and he constructed a telescope of that kind which still bears his name, and of which an ordinary opera-glass is an example. Within a few months he had produced instruments which were capable of magnifying thirty-two diameters, and within a year he had made and published observations on the solar spots, the lunar mountains, Jupiter's satellites, the phases of Venus, and Saturn's ring. Honours and emoluments were showered on him, and in 1610 he was enabled to give up his professorship and retire to Florence. In 1611 he paid a temporary visit to Rome, and exhibited in the gardens of the Vatican the new worlds revealed by the telescope.

It would seem that Galileo had always believed in the conjecture of Copernicus, published in 1543, that the earth and the planets revolved round the sun, but was afraid of promulgating it on account of the ridicule it excited. The existence of Jupiter's satellites seemed, however, to make its truth almost certain, and he now boldly preached it. The orthodox party resented his action, and on Feb. 24, 1616, the Inquisition declared that to suppose the sun the centre of the solar system was absurd, heretical, and contrary to Holy Scripture. The edict of March 5, 1616, which carried this into effect, has never been repealed though it has been long tacitly ignored : it is well known that the Jesuits evaded it by treating the theory as an hypothesis from which, though false, certain results would follow.

In 1632 Galileo published some dialogues on the system of the world in which he expounded the Copernican theory. In these, apparently through jealousy of Kepler's fame, he did not mention Kepler's laws, and he rejected Kepler's hypothesis that the tides are caused by the attraction of the moon. He rested the proof of the Copernican hypothesis on the absurd statement that it would cause tides, because different parts of the earth would rotate with different velocities. He was more successful in shewing that mechanical principles would account for the fact that a stone thrown straight up would fall again to the place from which it was thrown—a fact which had previously been one of the chief difficulties in the way of any theory which supposed the earth to be in motion.

The publication of this book was contrary to the edict of 1616. Galileo was at once summoned to Rome, forced to recant, do penance, and was released only on promise of obedience. The documents recently printed shew that he was threatened with the torture, but that there was no intention of carrying the threat into effect.

178. Galileo's work may I think be fairly summed up by saying that his researches on mechanics are deserving of high praise, and that they are memorable for clearly enunciating the fact that science must be founded on laws obtained by experiment; his astronomical observations and his deductions therefrom were also excellent, and were expounded with a literary skill which leaves nothing to be desired; but though he produced some of the evidence which placed the Copernican theory on a satisfactory basis, he did not himself make any special advance in the theory of astronomy.

179. **Revival of Interest in Pure Geometry.** The close of the sixteenth century was marked not only by the attempt to found a theory of dynamics based on laws derived from experiment, but also by a revived interest in geometry. This was largely due to the influence of Kepler.

180. **Kepler, 1571-1630.** Kepler, one of the founders of modern astronomy, was born of humble parents near Stuttgart; he was educated at Tübingen; in 1593 he was appointed professor at Grätz, where he made the acquaintance of a wealthy and beautiful widow whom he

married, but found too late that he had purchased his
freedom from pecuniary troubles at the expense of
domestic happiness. In 1599 he accepted an appointment as assistant to Tycho Brahe, and in 1601 succeeded
his master as astronomer to the emperor Rudolph II.
But his career was dogged by bad luck; first his stipend
was not paid; next his wife went mad and then died;
and though he married again in 1611 this proved an
even more unfortunate venture than before, for though,
to secure a better choice, he took the precaution to
make a preliminary selection of eleven girls whose
merits and demerits he carefully analysed in a paper
which is still extant, he finally selected a wrong one;
while to complete his discomfort he was expelled from
his chair, and narrowly escaped condemnation for hetero-
doxy. During this time he depended for his income on
telling fortunes and casting horoscopes, for, as he says,
"nature which has conferred upon every animal the
means of existence has designed astrology as an adjunct
and ally to astronomy." He seems, however, to have had
no scruple in charging heavily for his services, and to
the surprise of his contemporaries was found at his
death to have a considerable hoard of money. He died
while on a journey to try and recover for the benefit of
his children some of the arrears of his stipend.

181. Kepler's work in geometry consists rather in certain
general principles which he laid down and illustrated by
a few cases than in any systematic exposition of the
subject. In a short chapter on conics, published in 1604,
he enunciated what has been called the principle of continuity; and gave as an example the statement that a
parabola is at once the limiting case of an ellipse and of
a hyberbola; he illustrated the same doctrine by reference to the foci of conics (the word *focus* was introduced
by him); he also explained that parallel lines should be
regarded as meeting at infinity.

In his *Stereometria*, published in 1615, he determined the volumes of certain vessels and the areas of certain surfaces by means of infinitesimals or indivisibles instead of by the long and tedious method of exhaustions. The methods of Kepler are not altogether free from objection, but he was substantially correct, and by applying the law of continuity to infinitesimals he prepared the way for Cavalieri's method of indivisibles, and the infinitesimal calculus of Newton and Leibnitz.

182. I have already alluded to Kepler's advocacy of the use of logarithms. His work on astronomy lies outside the scope of this book. I will mention only that it was founded on the observations of Tycho Brahe, whose assistant he was. His three laws of planetary motion were the result of many and laborious efforts to reduce the phenomena of the solar system to certain simple rules. The first two were published in 1609, and stated that the planets describe ellipses round the sun, the sun being in a focus; and that the line joining the sun to any planet sweeps over equal areas in equal times. The third was published in 1619, and stated that the squares of the periodic times of the planets are proportional to the cubes of the major axes of their orbits.

183. **Desargues, 1593-1662.** While the conceptions of the geometry of the Greeks were being extended by Kepler, a Frenchman, whose name until recently was almost unknown, was inventing a new method of investigating the subject—a method which is now known as projective geometry. This was the discovery of Desargues. He was by profession an engineer and architect, but he gave some courses of gratuitous lectures in Paris from 1626 to about 1630 which made a great impression upon his contemporaries. The subject, however, soon fell into oblivion, chiefly because the analytical geometry of Descartes was so much more powerful as a

method of proof or discovery. Most of Desargues's researches were embodied in his *Brouillon proiect*, published in 1639, which contains the fundamental theorems on involution, homology, poles and polars, and perspective.

184. Mathematical Knowledge at the Close of the Renaissance. Thus by the beginning of the seventeenth century we may say that the principles of arithmetic, algebra, theory of equations, and trigonometry were expounded in a language and manner not very different from that now in use, and that the outlines of the subjects as we know them had been traced. Though much of the modern algebraical and trigonometrical notation had been introduced, it was not familiar to mathematicians, nor was it even universally accepted; and it was not until the end of the seventeenth century that the language of these subjects was definitely fixed.

If we turn to applied mathematics we find on the other hand that the science of statics had made but little advance in the eighteen centuries that had elapsed since the time of Archimedes, while the foundations of dynamics were laid by Galileo only at the close of the sixteenth century. In fact, as we shall see later, it was not until the time of Newton that the science of mechanics was placed on a satisfactory basis.

The Introduction of Modern Analysis.

185. Commencement of a New Era. The invention of analytical geometry and of the infinitesimal calculus may be taken as the commencement of a new era. The former was employed by Descartes in 1637; the latter was invented by Newton some thirty or forty years later. The science of mathematics subsequently is far more complex than in earlier periods: but for a couple of

centuries it may be generally described as characterized
by the development of analysis, and its application in particular to the phenomena of mechanics and astronomy.

186. **Descartes, 1596-1650.** Descartes was born near
Tours, and educated at the famous Jesuit school at la
Flêche. In 1612, on leaving it, he went to Paris to be
introduced to the world of fashion. At that time a man of
position usually entered either the army or the church;
Descartes chose the former, and in 1617 joined the army of
Prince Maurice of Orange then at Breda. Walking through
the streets there, he saw a placard in Dutch which excited
his curiosity, and stopping the first passer, he asked for a
translation. The placard was a challenge to all the world
to solve a certain geometrical problem, and Descartes
worked it out within a few hours. This unexpected test of
his mathematical attainments increased his distaste for a
military life, but under family influence and tradition he
remained for a few years in the army. However, in 1621
he resigned his commission, and spent the next five years
in travel and the study of mathematics.

In 1626 he took up his residence at Paris, where he is
described by a contemporary as "a little well-built figure,
modestly clad in green taffety, and only wearing sword and
feather in token of his quality as a gentleman." Two years
later he moved to Holland to secure more leisure. . There
for the next twenty years he lived, giving up his time to
philosophy and mathematics. Science, he says, may be
compared to a tree, metaphysics is the root, physics is the
trunk, and the three chief branches are mechanics, medicine, and morals, these forming the three applications of
our knowledge, namely, to the external world, to the
human body, and to the conduct of life: and with these
subjects alone his writings are concerned. He spent the
commencement of his stay in Holland in an attempt to
frame a physical theory of the universe; but finding that
its publication was likely to bring on him the hostility

of the church, and having no desire to pose as a martyr, he abandoned it. He then devoted himself to composing a treatise on universal science ; this was published at Leyden in 1637 under the title *Discours de la méthode pour bien conduire sa raison et chercher la verité dans les sciences,* and to it were added three appendices entitled *La Dioptrique,* *Les Météores,* and *La Géométrie*: it is from the last of these that the invention of analytical geometry dates. In 1649 he went to Sweden on the invitation of the Queen, and died a few months later of inflammation of the lungs.

In appearance, Descartes was a small man with large head, projecting brow, prominent nose, and black hair coming down to his eyebrows. In disposition he was cold and selfish. Considering the range of his studies he was by no means widely read, and he despised both learning and art unless something tangible could be extracted therefrom.

187. Descartes's philosophical theories do not concern us here. His chief contributions to mathematics were his analytical geometry and his theory of vortices, and it is on his researches in connection with the former of these subjects that his reputation rests.

188. In analytical geometry Descartes was the first to indicate that a point in a plane could be completely determined if its distances, say x and y, from two fixed lines drawn at right angles in the plane were given, with the convention familiar to us as to the interpretation of positive and negative values; and that though an equation $f(x, y) = 0$ was indeterminate and could be satisfied by an infinite number of values of x and y, yet these values of x and y determined the coordinates of a number of points which form a curve of which the equation $f(x, y) = 0$ expresses some geometrical property, that is, a property true of the curve at every point on it. Descartes asserted that a point in space could be

similarly determined by three coordinates, but he confined his attention to plane curves.

It was at once seen that in order to investigate the
properties of a curve it was sufficient to select any characteristic geometrical property as a definition, and to
express it by means of an equation between the (current)
coordinates of any point on the curve, that is, to translate the definition into the language of analytical geometry.
The equation so obtained contains implicitly every property of the curve, and any particular property can be
deduced from it by ordinary algebra without troubling
about the geometry of the figure. I need not go further into details, for every one to whom the above is
intelligible will appreciate the value of the method.

189. Descartes's *Géométrie* is divided into three books.
The first book commences with an explanation of the
principles of analytical geometry, and contains a discussion
of a certain problem which had been propounded by
Pappus, of which the most important case is to find the
locus of a point such that the product of the perpendiculars on two given straight lines shall be in a constant
ratio to the product of the perpendiculars on two other
given straight lines. Pappus had stated that the locus
was a conic, but he gave no proof; Descartes also failed
to prove this by pure geometry, but he shewed that the
curve was represented by an equation of the second degree, that is, was a conic; subsequently Newton gave
an elegant solution by pure geometry. In the second
book Descartes discussed some problems concerning particular curves, and their tangents and normals.

190. The third book of the *Géométrie* contains an analysis
of the algebra then current. It has affected the language
of the subject by fixing the custom of employing the
letters at the beginning of the alphabet to denote known
quantities, and those at the end of the alphabet to denote
unknown quantities, and it has brought into general use

the system of indices now adopted. In this book Descartes applied his rule for finding a limit to the number of positive and of negative roots of an algebraical equation. He introduced the method of indeterminate coefficients for the solution of equations, and he believed that he had given a method by which equations of any order could be solved, but in this he was mistaken.

191. Of the two other appendices to the *Discours*, one was devoted to optics. The chief interest of this consists in the statement given of the law of refraction. Descartes here discussed the best shape for the lenses of a telescope. He seems to have been doubtful whether to regard the rays of light as proceeding from the eye and so to speak touching the object, as the Greeks had done, or as proceeding from the object and so affecting the eye; but, since he considered the velocity of light to be infinite, he did not deem the point particularly important. The other appendix contains an explanation of certain atmospheric phenomena, including the rainbow; Descartes was unacquainted with the unequal refrangibility of rays of light of different colours, and the explanation of the latter is necessarily incomplete.

192. Descartes's physical theory of the universe rests on the assumption that the matter of the universe is in motion, and that the motion must result in a number of vortices. He stated that the sun is the centre of an immense whirlpool of this matter, in which the planets float and are swept round like straws in a whirlpool of water. Each planet is supposed to be the centre of a secondary whirlpool by which its satellites are carried : these secondary whirlpools are supposed to produce variations of density in the surrounding medium which constitute the primary whirlpool, and so cause the planets to move in ellipses and not in circles. These assumptions are unsupported by investigation. It is not difficult to prove that on his hypotheses the sun would be in the

centre of these ellipses and not at a focus (as Kepler had shewn was the case), and that the weight of a body at every place on the surface of the earth except the equator would act in a direction which was not vertical. Still, in spite of its crudeness and its inherent defects, the theory of vortices marks a fresh era in astronomy, for it was an attempt to explain the phenomena of the whole universe by the same mechanical laws which experiment shews to be true on the earth.

193. **Cavalieri, 1598-1647.** Almost contemporaneously with the publication in 1637 of Descartes's geometry, the principles of the integral calculus, so far as they are concerned with summation, were being worked out in Italy. This was effected by what was called the principle of indivisibles, and was the invention of Cavalieri, a professor of mathematics at Bologna. He applied it to problems connected with the quadrature of curves and surfaces, the determination of volumes, and the positions of centres of gravity, and it at once almost entirely superseded the tedious methods of exhaustions used by the Greeks. In principle the methods are the same, but the notation of indivisibles is more concise and convenient. It was in its turn superseded at the beginning of the eighteenth century by the integral calculus.

194. The principle of indivisibles had been used by Kepler in 1604 and 1615 in a somewhat crude form, but it was first explicitly stated by Cavalieri in 1629, though not published till 1635. The method of indivisibles is simply that any magnitude may be divided into an infinite number of small quantities which can be made to bear any required ratios (*e.g.* equality) one to the other. One example will suffice. Suppose it be required to find the area of a right-angled triangle. Let the base be made up of n indivisibles (or points) and the other side of na indivisibles, then the ordinates at the successive points of the base will contain a, $2a$, ..., na indivisibles. Therefore

F

the number of indivisibles in the area is $a + 2a + \ldots + na$; the sum of which is $\frac{1}{2}n^2a + \frac{1}{2}na$. Since n is very large, we may neglect $\frac{1}{2}na$ as inconsiderable compared with $\frac{1}{2}n^2a$, and the area is $\frac{1}{2}(na)n$, that is, $\frac{1}{2} \times$ altitude $\times$ base. There is no difficulty in criticizing such a proof, but, although the form in which it is presented is indefensible, the substance is correct.

It would be misleading to give the above as the only example of the method, and therefore, to illustrate its application as modified and corrected by *the method of limits*, I proceed to find the area outside a parabola APC, and bounded by the curve, the tangent at A, and a diameter DC. Complete the parallelogram $ABCD$. Divide AD into n equal parts, let AM contain r of them, and let

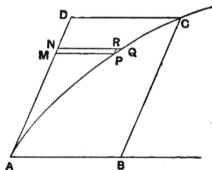

MN be the $(r+1)$th part. Draw MP and NQ parallel to AB, and draw PR parallel to AD. Then, when n becomes indefinitely large, the curvilinear area $APCD$ will be the limit of the sum of all parallelograms like PN. Now

area PN : area $BD = MP \cdot MN : DC \cdot AD$.

But $MN : AD = 1 : n$, and, by the properties of the parabola, $MP : DC = AM^2 : AD^2 = r^2 : n^2$.

Hence $MP \cdot MN : DC \cdot AD = r^2 : n^3$,

$\therefore$ area PN : area $BD = r^2 : n^3$.

Therefore, ultimately,

$$\frac{\text{area } APCD}{\text{area } BD} = \frac{1^2 + 2^2 + \ldots + (n-1)^2}{n^3} = \frac{\frac{1}{6}n(n-1)(2n-1)}{n^3} = \frac{1}{3}\left(1 - \frac{1}{n}\right)\left(1 - \frac{1}{2n}\right) = \frac{1}{3}.$$

195. **Pascal, 1623-1662.** Among the contemporaries of Descartes none displayed greater natural genius than Pascal. He shewed exceptional precocity as a boy, and to ensure his not being overworked, he was brought up at home. His education was at first confined to the study of languages, and he was forbidden to read any mathematics: this naturally excited his curiosity, and one day, being then twelve years old, he asked in what geometry consisted. His tutor replied that it was the science of constructing exact figures and of determining the proportions between their different parts. Pascal, stimulated no doubt by the injunction against reading it, gave up his play-time to this new study, and in a few weeks had discovered for himself many properties of figures, and in particular the proposition that the sum of the angles of a triangle is equal to two right angles. His father struck by this display of ability, allowed him to begin mathematics, wherein he made rapid progress.

At the age of fourteen he was admitted to the weekly meetings of French geometricians, from which the French Academy ultimately sprung. At sixteen he wrote an essay on conic sections; at eighteen he constructed the first arithmetical machine, an instrument which eight years later he further improved and patented; and his correspondence with Fermat about this time shews that he was then turning his attention to analytical geometry and physics.

In 1650, when in the midst of these researches, Pascal suddenly abandoned his favourite pursuits to study religion, or as he says in his *Pensées* "to contemplate the greatness and the misery of man," but three years later, when he had to administer his father's estate, he returned to the study of mathematics and science. Towards the end of 1654, he was driving a four-in-hand, when the horses ran away; the leaders dashed over the parapet of the bridge at Neuilly, and Pascal was saved only by the traces breaking. Always somewhat of a mystic, he considered this a special summons to abandon the world; he wrote an account of the accident on a small piece of parchment, which for the rest of his life he wore next to his heart to remind him of his covenant. He then moved to Port Royal, where he continued to live until his death. Always delicate, he had injured his health by his incessant study, and from the age of seventeen or eighteen he suffered constantly from insomnia and acute dyspepsia.

196. His early essay on the geometry of conics, written in 1639 but not published till 1779, seems to have been founded on the teaching of Desargues. Two of the results are important as well as interesting. The first of these is the theorem known now as "Pascal's theorem," namely, that if a hexagon be inscribed in a conic, the points of intersection of the opposite sides will lie in a straight line. The second, which is really due to Desargues, is that if a quadrilateral be inscribed in a conic, and a straight line be drawn cutting the sides taken in order in the points A, B, C, and D, and the conic in P and Q, then

$$PA \cdot PC : PB \cdot PD = QA \cdot QC : QB \cdot QD.$$

197. Pascal's Arithmetical Triangle was written in 1653, but not printed till 1665. The triangle can be easily written down, and the numbers in any diagonal give the coefficients of the expansion of a binomial: moreover the construction enables us to write down the expansion of $(a+b)^n$ if that of $(a+b)^{n-1}$ be known. Pascal used the triangle partly for this purpose and partly to find the numbers of combinations of m things taken n at a time, which he stated (correctly) to be $(n+1)(n+2)(n+3)...m/(m-n)!$

198. Perhaps as a mathematician Pascal is best known in connection with his correspondence with Fermat in 1654, in which he laid down the principles of the theory

of probabilities. This correspondence arose from a problem proposed by a gamester, the Chevalier de Méré, to Pascal, who communicated it to Fermat. The problem was this. Two players of equal skill want to leave the table before finishing their game. Their scores and the number of points which constitute the game being given, it is desired to find in what proportion they should divide the stakes. Pascal and Fermat agreed on the answer, but gave different proofs. Pascal's solution is long, but the principle of it may be gathered from his discussion of the simple case where two players of equal skill, A and B, play a game of three points, each staking thirty-two pistoles, and where A has gained two points and B one point. Then if B win the next point, they are on terms of equality, and if they leave off playing each ought to take thirty-two pistoles. But if A win the next point, he gets sixty-four pistoles and B gets none. Thus, if A wins, sixty-four pistoles belong to him, and, if he loses, then thirty-two pistoles belong to him. If, therefore, A and B wish to separate without playing again, A would say to B, "I am certain of thirty-two pistoles even if I lose this game, and as for the other thirty-two pistoles perhaps I shall have them and perhaps you will have them; the chances are equal. Let us then divide these thirty-two pistoles equally, and give me also the thirty-two pistoles of which I am certain." Thus A will have forty-eight pistoles and B sixteen pistoles. Pascal solved the similar problem when the game is won by whoever first obtains $m+n$ points, and one player has m while the other has n points.

199. The last mathematical work of Pascal was that on the cycloid. The cycloid is the curve traced out by a point on the circumference of a circular hoop which rolls along a straight line. Galileo, in 1630, had called attention to this curve. Four years later Roberval found

its area. Several questions connected with it, and with the surface and volume generated by its revolution about its axis, base, or the tangent at its vertex, were then proposed. These and some analogous problems, as well as the positions of the centres of gravity of the solids formed, were solved by Pascal in 1658, and the results were issued as a challenge to the world. Wallis succeeded in solving all the questions except those connected with the centres of gravity. Pascal's own solutions were effected by the method of indivisibles, and are similar to those which a modern mathematician would give by the aid of the integral calculus. He obtained by summation what are equivalent to the integrals of $\sin \phi$, $\sin^2 \phi$, and $\phi \sin \phi$, one limit being either 0 or $\frac{1}{2}\pi$.

200. **Wallis, 1616-1703.** Wallis was the eldest son of the vicar of Ashford, a man in easy circumstances. The boy was sent to Felstead school, and one day, in his holidays, when fifteen years old, he happened to see a book of arithmetic in the hands of his brother; struck with curiosity at the odd signs and symbols in it he borrowed the book, and in a fortnight, with his brother's help, had mastered the subject. As it was intended that he should be a doctor, he went to Cambridge, and while there he kept an "act" on the doctrine of the circulation of the blood—this is said to have been the first occasion in Europe on which this theory was publicly maintained in a disputation. His interests, however, centred on mathematics. On the whole he adhered to the Puritan party, to whom he rendered great assistance in deciphering the royalist despatches; but he took orders, and he joined the moderate Presbyterians in signing the remonstrance against the execution of Charles I., by which he incurred the lasting hostility of the Independents. In spite of their opposition, he was appointed in 1649 to the Savilian chair of geometry at Oxford, where he lived until his death in 1703. His mathematical

works are notable partly for the introduction of the use
of infinite series as an ordinary part of analysis, and
partly for the fact that they revealed and explained
to all students the principles of the new methods of
analysis introduced by his contemporaries and immediate
predecessors. He also wrote on theology, logic, and
philosophy; and was the first to devise a system for
teaching deaf-mutes.

201. The most important of Wallis's works was his
Arithmetica Infinitorum, published in 1656. In this
treatise the methods of analysis of Descartes and Cavalieri
were systematized and extended, but the exposition is
open to criticism. He commenced by proving the law
of indices ;- shewed that x^0, x^{-1}, x^{-2}, ..., represent 1, $1/x$,
$1/x^2$, ... ; that $x^{\frac{1}{2}}$ represents the square root of x, that $x^{\frac{2}{3}}$
represents the cube root of x^2, and generally that x^{-n}
represents the reciprocal of x^n and that $x^{p/q}$ represents
the qth root of x^p. He next, by the method of indivisibles, found the area enclosed between the curve
$y = x^m$, the axis of x, and any ordinate $x = h$; and shewed
that similar results might be written down for any curve
of the form $y = \Sigma a x^m$: and hence that, if the ordinate y
of a curve can be expanded in powers of the abscissa x,
its quadrature can be determined.

202. Three years later Wallis published a tract containing the solution of the problems on the cycloid which had
been proposed by Pascal. In this he explained how the
principles laid down in his *Arithmetica Infinitorum* could be
used for the rectification of algebraic curves ; and gave
a solution of the problem to rectify the semi-cubical
parabola $x^3 = ay^2$, which had been discovered in 1657 by
his pupil William Neil. This was the first case in which
the length of a curved line was determined by mathematics, and since all attempts to rectify the ellipse and
hyperbola had been (necessarily) ineffectual, it had been
previously supposed that no curves could be rectified, as

indeed Descartes had definitely asserted to be the case. The cycloid was the second curve rectified ; this was done by Wren in 1658. Early in 1658 a similar discovery, independent of that of Neil, was made by van Heuraët, and this was published by van Schooten in 1659 in his edition of Descartes's *Géométrie*.

203. **Fermat, 1601-1665.** While Descartes was laying the foundations of analytical geometry, the same subject was occupying the attention of another and hardly less distinguished Frenchman. Fermat, who was born near Montauban, was the son of a leather merchant; he was educated at home ; in 1631 he obtained the post of councillor for the local parliament at Toulouse, and he discharged the duties of the office with scrupulous accuracy and fidelity. There, devoting most of his leisure to mathematics, he spent the remainder of his life. Except a few isolated papers Fermat published nothing in his lifetime, and gave no systematic exposition of his methods.

204. The theory of numbers appears to have been his favourite study. The following examples will illustrate the nature of his investigations.

(i) If p be a prime and a be prime to p, then $a^{p-1} - 1$ is divisible by p.

(ii) A prime (greater than 2) can be expressed as the difference of two square integers in one and only one way.

(iii) Every prime of the form $4n + 1$ is expressible, and that in one way only, as the sum of two squares.

(iv) No integral values of x, y, z can be found to satisfy the equation $x^n + y^n = z^n$, if n be an integer greater than 2. This proposition has acquired extraordinary celebrity from the fact that no general demonstration of it has been given, but there is no reason to doubt that it is true.

205. It would seem from Fermat's correspondence that (independently of Descartes, and perhaps as early as 1628) he had thought out the principles of analytical geometry, and had realized that from the equation (or as he calls it,

the "specific property") of a curve all its properties could be deduced, but these views were not made public till some time after 1637. Fermat's extant papers on geometry deal mainly with the application of infinitesimals, to the determination of the tangents to curves, to the quadrature of curves, and to questions of maxima and minima.

206. Fermat shares with Pascal the honour of having created the theory of probabilities. I have already mentioned (see above, art. 198) the problem proposed to Pascal, and which he communicated to Fermat, and have there indicated Pascal's solution. Fermat's solution depends on the theory of combinations, and will be sufficiently illustrated by the case of two players A and B, where A wants two points to win and B three points. The game will be then certainly decided in the course of four trials. Take the letters a and b and write down all the combinations that can be formed of four letters. These combinations are 16 in number, namely *aaaa, aaab, aaba, aabb*; *abaa, abab, abba, abbb*; *baaa, baab, baba, babb*; *bbaa, bbab, bbba, bbbb*. Now every combination in which a occurs twice or oftener represents a case favourable to A, and every combination in which b occurs three times or oftener represents a case favourable to B. Thus, on counting them, it will be found that there are 11 cases favourable to A, and 5 cases favourable to B; and, since these cases are all equally likely, A's chance of winning the game is to B's chance as 11 is to 5.

207. Fermat's reputation is unique in the history of science. The problems on numbers which he had proposed long defied all efforts to solve them, and many of them yielded only to the skill of Euler. One still remains unsolved. This extraordinary achievement has overshadowed his other work, but in fact it is all of the highest order of excellence, and we can only regret that he thought fit to write so little.

208. **Huygens, 1629-1695.** The life of the great Dutch

mathematician was uneventful, and is a mere record of his various memoirs and researches. His most important work was his *Horologium Oscillatorium*, published in 1673. The first chapter is devoted to pendulum clocks, which he had invented in 1656: the time-pieces previously in use being balance-clocks. The second chapter contains a complete account of the descent of heavy bodies under their own weights in a vacuum, either vertically down or on smooth curves: he shewed here that the cycloid is tautochronous. In the third chapter he defined evolutes and involutes, proved some of their more elementary properties, and illustrated his methods by finding the evolutes of the cycloid and the parabola: these are the earliest instances in which the envelope of a moving line was determined. In the fourth chapter he solved the problem of the compound pendulum, and shewed that the centres of oscillation and suspension are interchangeable. In the fifth and last chapter he discussed again the theory of clocks, pointed out that if the bob of the pendulum were made by means of cycloidal checks to oscillate in a cycloid the oscillations would be isochronous; and finished by shewing that the centrifugal force on a body which moves round a circle of radius r with a uniform velocity v varies directly as v^2 and inversely as r. This work contains the first attempt to apply dynamics to bodies of finite size and not merely to particles.

209. In 1689 he came from Holland to England in order to make the acquaintance of Newton, whose *Principia* had been published in 1687, the extraordinary merits of which Huygens had at once recognized. On his return he published his treatise on light, in which the undulatory theory was expounded. According to this theory space is filled with an extremely rare ether, and light is caused by a series of waves in the ether which are set in motion by the pulsations of the luminous body. From this hypothesis Huygens deduced the laws of reflection and refraction, ex-

plained the phenomena of double refraction, and gave a construction for the extraordinary ray in biaxal crystals.

210. **Other Mathematicians of This Time.** As we approach modern times the history of mathematics becomes more complex, and the number of those who studied it becomes much greater. Several writers of the early half of the seventeenth century might be mentioned who extended the bounds of the subject, and who prepared the way for the discoveries of their successors. Here I can do no more than mention the names of *Mersenne*, 1588-1648; *van Schooten*, who died in 1661; *Hudde*, 1633-1704; *Nicholas Mercator*, who died in 1687; *Barrow*, 1630-1677, the predecessor of Newton in the Lucasian professorship at Cambridge; *Viscount Brouncker*, 1620-1684, who familiarized the public with the use of continued fractions, which had been introduced by Cataldi in 1613; *James Gregory*, 1638-1675, the inventor of the reflecting telescope; and *De la Hire*, 1640-1719.

211. **Newton, 1642-1727.** Newton was born in Lincolnshire. He was educated at Trinity College, Cambridge, and lived there from 1661 till 1696, during which time he produced the bulk of his mathematical work. In 1696 he was appointed to a valuable government office, and moved to London, where he resided till his death. His extraordinary abilities enabled him to advance every branch of mathematical science then studied, as well as to create some new subjects.

212. He knew no mathematics when he came to Cambridge, but within four years he was an accomplished mathematician. An extant manuscript, dated May 28, 1665, written in the same year as that in which he received his B.A. degree, contains the earliest statement of his invention of fluxions. It was about the same time that he discovered the binomial theorem. The next year and a half were crowded with brilliant discoveries. In them he worked out the fluxional calculus tolerably com-

pletely; he devised instruments for grinding lenses to particular forms other than spherical; perhaps he decomposed solar light into different colours; and he thought out the fundamental principles of his theory of gravitation.

213. Leaving out details, his reasoning at this time (1666) on gravitation seems to have been as follows. He knew that gravity extended to the tops of the highest hills, and he conjectured that it might extend as far as the moon, and be the force which retained the moon in its orbit about the earth. To verify this hypothesis he proceeded thus. He knew that if a stone were allowed to fall near the surface of the earth, the attraction of the earth (that is, the weight of the stone) caused it to move

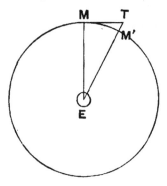

through 16 feet in one second. The moon's orbit relative to the earth is nearly a circle; and as a rough approximation taking it to be so, he knew the distance of the moon, and therefore the length of its path; he also knew the time the moon took to go once round it, namely, a month. Hence he could easily find its velocity at any point such as M. He could therefore find the distance MT through which it would move in one second, if it were not pulled by the earth's attraction. At the end of that second it was, however, at M', and therefore the earth must have pulled it through the distance TM' in one second (assuming the direction of the earth's pull to be constant). Now he had already reasoned that, if Kepler's third law were rigorously true, the attraction of the earth on a body would decrease as the body was removed farther away from the earth in a proportion inversely as the square of the distance from the centre of the earth. If this were the actual law, and gravity were the sole force which retained the moon in its orbit, then TM' should be to 16 feet in a proportion which was inversely as the square of the distance of the moon from the centre of the earth to the square of the radius of the earth. In 1679, when he repeated the investigation, TM' was found to have the value which was required by the hypothesis, and the verification was complete; but in 1666 his estimate of the distance of the moon was inaccurate, and when he made the calculation he found that TM' was about one-eighth less than it ought to have been on his hypothesis. This discrepancy did not shake his faith in the belief that gravity extended to the moon and varied inversely as the square of the distance, but it would seem that he inferred that some other force —probably Descartes's vortices—acted on the moon as well as gravity.

214. In 1667 Newton was elected to a fellowship at his college, and permanently took up his residence at Cambridge; two years later Barrow resigned the Lucasian chair in his favour. While he held the professorship, it was Newton's practice to lecture publicly once a week in one term of each year, probably dictating his lectures as rapidly as they could be taken down; and in the week following the lecture to devote four hours to appointments which he gave to students who wished to come to his rooms to discuss the results of the previous lecture. He never repeated a course, and generally the lectures of one course began from the point at which the preceding course had ended. The manuscripts of his lectures for seventeen out of the first eighteen years of his tenure of the chair are extant.

215. When first appointed, Newton chose optics for the subject of his lectures and researches, and before the end of 1669 he had worked out the details of his discovery of the decomposition of a ray of white light into rays of different colours by means of a prism, from which the explanation of the phenomenon of the rainbow followed. By a curious chapter of accidents he failed to correct the chromatic aberration of two colours by means of a couple of prisms: hence he abandoned the hope of making a refracting telescope which should be achromatic, and instead designed a reflecting telescope. In 1672 he invented a reflecting microscope, and somewhat later he invented the sextant.

216. Newton next set himself to examine the problem as to how light was produced, and by the end of 1675 he had worked out the corpuscular or emission theory. Only three ways have been suggested in which light can be produced mechanically. Either the eye may be supposed to send out something which, so to speak, feels the object (as the Greeks believed); or the object perceived may send out something which hits or affects the eye (as assumed in the emission theory); or there may be some medium between the eye and the object, and the object may cause some change in the form or condition of this medium and thus affect the eye (as supposed in the wave or undulatory theory). The emission and wave theories account for all the obvious phenomena of geometrical optics such as reflection, refraction, etc. The Newtonian theory is now known to be untenable, but it should be noted that Newton always treated it as a mere hypothesis from which certain results would follow: it would seem that he believed the wave theory to be intrinsically more probable, and it was the difficulty of explaining diffraction on that theory that led him to suggest another hypothesis.

217. Two letters written by Newton in 1676 are interesting as giving an account of the history of his methods

of analysis.   In answer to a request from Leibnitz, Newton wrote on June 13, 1676, giving a brief account of his methods of expanding functions in series, adding the binomial theorem, the expansions of $\sin^{-1}x$, and of $\sin x$, and an expression for the rectification of an elliptic arc in an infinite series.   In a second explanatory letter, dated October 24, 1676, Newton said that altogether he had used three methods for expansion in series.   His first was arrived at by considering the series of expressions $(1-x^2)^{\frac{0}{2}}$, $(1-x^2)^2$, $(1-x^2)^{\frac{6}{2}}$, ..., from which he deduced by interpolations the law which connects the successive coefficients in the expansions of $(1-x^2)^{\frac{1}{2}}$, $(1-x^2)^{\frac{3}{2}}$, ...; and thus obtained the expression for the general term in the expansion of a binomial, *i.e.* the binomial theorem, a conclusion which he verified in several ways.   Having established this result, he then (before 1665-6) discarded the method of interpolation in series, and employed his binomial theorem to express (when possible) the ordinate of a curve in an infinite series in ascending powers of the abscissa, and thus by Wallis's method he obtained expressions in an infinite series for the areas and arcs of curves.   He next explained that he had also a third method, of which he had (about 1669) sent an account to Barrow and Collins, illustrated by applications to areas, rectification, cubature, etc.   This was the method of fluxions; but Newton gave no description of it here, though he added some illustrations of its use and a list of forms which are immediately integrable. The first illustration is on the quadrature of the curve represented by the equation $y = ax^m(b+cx^n)^p$.

Leibnitz, in replying, explained his method of determining tangents to curves, "not by fluxions of lines but by the differences of numbers"; and he introduced his notation of dx and dy for the infinitesimal differences between the coordinates of two consecutive points on a curve.   He also gave a solution of the problem to find a curve whose subtangent is constant, which shews that he could integrate.

218. In 1679 Hooke, at the request of the Royal Society, wrote to Newton expressing a hope that he would make further communications to the Society, and in the course of the letter mentioned Picard's geodetical researches, in which a substantially correct value of the radius of the earth had been used. This led Newton to repeat, with Picard's data, his calculations of 1666 on the lunar orbit, and he found the verification of his former hypothesis on gravitation (see above, art. 213) was complete. He then proceeded to the general theory of motion under a centripetal force, and demonstrated (i) the equable description of areas ; (ii) that if an ellipse were described about a focus under a centripetal force, the law was that of the inverse square of the distance ; (iii) and conversely, that the orbit of a particle projected under the influence of such a force was a conic. Following his custom of publishing nothing which could land him in a scientific controversy, these results were locked up in his note-books, and it was only a specific question addressed to him five years later that led to their publication.

219. The *Universal Arithmetic*, which is on algebra, theory of equations, and miscellaneous problems, contains the substance of Newton's lectures during the years 1673 to 1683. In them he introduced the system of literal indices. He explained that the equation whose roots are the solution of a given problem will have as many roots as there are different possible cases ; and he considered how it happened that the equation to which a problem led might contain roots which did not satisfy the original question. He extended Descartes's rule of signs to give limits to the number of imaginary roots. He gave rules to find a superior limit to the positive roots of a numerical equation, and to determine the approximate values of the numerical roots. He also enunciated the theorem known

by his name for finding the sum of the nth powers of the roots of an equation, and laid the foundation of the theory of symmetrical functions of the roots of an equation.

220. In August, 1684, Halley came to Cambridge in order to ask Newton what the orbit of a planet would be if the law of attraction were that of the inverse square as was commonly suspected to be approximately the case. Newton immediately asserted that it was an ellipse, and promised to send or write out afresh the demonstration of it which he had found in 1679. This was sent in November, 1684, and Halley, at once recognizing the importance of the communication, again went to Cambridge, and induced Newton to undertake to attack the whole problem of gravitation, and to publish his results.

It would seem that Newton had long believed that every particle of matter attracts every other particle, and that he suspected that the attraction varied as the product of their masses and inversely as the square of the distance between them: but it is certain that he did not then know what the attraction of a spherical mass on any external point would be, and did not think it likely that a particle would be attracted by the earth as if the latter were concentrated into a single particle at its centre. Hence he must have thought that his discoveries of 1679 were only approximately true when applied to the solar system. His mathematical analysis, however, now shewed that the sun and planets, regarded as spheres, exerted their attractions as if their masses were collected at their centres, and thus his former results were absolutely true of the solar system, save only for a correction caused by the slight deviation of the sun, earth, and planets, from a perfectly spherical form.

221. The first book of the *Principia* was finished before the summer of 1685. It is given up to the consideration of the motion of particles or bodies in free space either

in known orbits, or under the action of known forces, or under their mutual attraction. In it Newton expounded the law of attraction that every particle of matter in the universe attracts every other particle with a force which varies directly as the product of their masses.and inversely as the square of the distance between them; and the law of attraction for spherical shells of constant density is thence deduced. The book is prefaced by an introduction on the science of dynamics.

The second book of the *Principia* was completed in 1686. This book treats of motion in a resisting medium. The theory of hydrodynamics was here created, and it was applied to the phenomena of waves, tides, and acoustics. Newton concluded it by shewing that the Cartesian theory of vortices was inconsistent both with the known facts and with the laws of motion.

In the third book, the theorems of the first book are applied to the chief phenomena of the solar system, the masses and distances of the planets and (whenever sufficient data existed) of their satellites are determined. In particular the motion of the moon, the various inequalities therein, and the theory of the tides are worked out in detail and as fully as was then possible. Newton also investigated the theory of comets, shewed that they belong to the solar system, and illustrated his results by considering certain special comets. The complete work was published in 1687.

222. The demonstrations throughout are geometrical, but are rendered unnecessarily difficult by their conciseness and by the absence of any clue to the method by which they were obtained. The reason why the arguments were presented in a geometrical form appears to have been that the infinitesimal calculus was then unknown, and, had Newton used it to demonstrate results which were in themselves opposed to the prevalent philosophy of the time, the controversy as to the truth of his results

would have been hampered by a dispute concerning the validity of the methods used in proving them.

223. I need not pursue Newton's scientific career further. In 1696 he was appointed Warden of the Mint, and moved to London, and in 1699 was made Master of the Mint. His treatise on optics, his essay on analytical geometry applied to cubic curves (wherein many of the fundamental properties of asymptotes, multiple points and isolated loops of curves were established), and his exposition of the fluxional calculus were published in 1704 ; and other works followed later.

224. The fluxional calculus is one form of the infinitesimal calculus expressed in a certain notation, just as the differential calculus is another aspect of the same calculus expressed in a different notation ; but for most purposes the notation of the fluxional calculus is less convenient than that of the differential calculus. The latter notation was invented by Leibnitz in 1675, and published in 1684 some nine years before the earliest printed account of Newton's method of fluxions. But the question whether the general idea of the calculus expressed in that notation was obtained by Leibnitz from Newton or whether it was invented independently gave rise to a long and bitter controversy. The question is one of difficulty, but I think the evidence leads to the conclusion that Leibnitz obtained the idea of the differential calculus from a manuscript of Newton's which he saw in 1675.

225. In appearance Newton was short but well set, with a square lower jaw, brown eyes, a broad forehead, and rather sharp features. His hair turned grey before he was thirty, and remained thick and white as silver till his death. In his dress he was slovenly. He was often so absorbed in his own thoughts as to be anything but a lively companion. He was straightforward, scrupulously honest, and deeply religious, having, as Bishop Burnet said, "the whitest soul" he ever knew.

226. His name remains the greatest in the history of mathematics, and we still wonder at the record of what he accomplished.   He modestly attributed his discoveries largely to the admirable work done by his predecessors; and once explained that, if he had seen farther than other men, it was only because he had stood on the shoulders of giants.   He summed up his own estimate of his work by saying, " I do not know what I may appear to the world ; but to myself I seem to have been only like a boy, playing on the sea-shore, and diverting myself, in now and then finding a smoother pebble, or a prettier shell than ordinary, whilst the great ocean of truth lay all undiscovered before me."   He was morbidly sensitive to being involved in any discussions.   I believe that, with the exception of his papers on optics, every one of his works was published only under pressure from his friends and against his own wishes.

227. **Introduction of the Calculus on the Continent.** Modern analysis is not derived directly from Newton, but rather from the works of Leibnitz and the Bernoullis : these I will now briefly describe.

228. **Leibnitz, 1646-1716.** Leibnitz was born at Leipzig. His father died before he was six, and the teaching at the school to which he was then sent was inefficient, but his industry triumphed over all difficulties ; by the time he was twelve he had taught himself to read Latin easily, and had begun Greek ; and before he was twenty he had mastered the ordinary text-books on mathematics, philosophy, theology, and law.   Refused the degree of Doctor of Laws at Leipzig by those who were jealous of his youth and learning, he moved to Nuremberg ; and an essay which he there wrote on the study of law led to an appointment in the diplomatic service.   The violent seizure of various small places in Alsace in 1670 excited universal alarm in Germany as to the designs of Louis XIV. ; and Leibnitz drew up a scheme by which it was proposed to

offer German co-operation, if France liked to take Egypt
and use the possession of that country as a basis for attack
against Holland in Asia, on condition that Germany was
to be left undisturbed by France.   This bears a curious
resemblance to the similar plan by which Napoleon I. proposed to attack England.   In 1672 Leibnitz went to Paris
on the invitation of the French government to explain the
details of the scheme, but nothing came of it.

229. At Paris he met Huygens, whose conversation led
him to study geometry and commence his mathematical
researches.   In 1674 he entered the service of the Brunswick family ; in 1676 he visited London ; and then moved
to Hanover, where till his death he occupied the well-paid
post of ducal librarian.   The last years of his life—from
1709 to 1716—were embittered by the controversy as to
whether he had discovered the differential calculus independently of Newton's previous investigations or whether
he had derived the fundamental idea from Newton and
merely invented another notation for it.

230. Leibnitz was overfond of money and personal distinctions ; was unscrupulous, as might be expected from a
professional diplomatist of that time ; but possessed singularly attractive manners, and those who once came under
the charm of his personal presence remained sincerely
attached to him.   His mathematical reputation was largely
augmented by the eminent position that he occupied in
diplomacy, philosophy, and literature ; and the power
thence derived was increased by his influence in the
management of the *Acta Eruditorum*, which was then the
only private scientific journal of any importance.

231. The only mathematical papers of first-rate importance which he produced are those on the differential
calculus.   The earliest of these was one published in 1684,
in which he enunciated a general method for finding
maxima and minima, and for drawing tangents to curves.
One inverse problem, namely, to find the curve whose sub-

tangent is constant, was also discussed. The notation is the same as that with which we are familiar, and the differential coefficients of x^n, and of products and quotients were determined. In 1686 and 1694 he wrote papers on the principles of the new calculus. In these his statements of the objects and methods of the infinitesimal calculus are somewhat obscure, and his attempt to place the subject on a metaphysical basis did not tend to clearness; but the notation he introduced is superior to that of Newton, and the fact that all the results of modern mathematics are expressed in the language invented by Leibnitz has proved the best monument of his work.

232. Leibnitz wrote several papers on questions about curves and on mechanical problems. These exhibit skill in analysis, but when he leaves his symbols and attempts to interpret his results he frequently commits blunders. In spite of this, his title to fame rests on a sure basis, for, by his advocacy of the differential calculus, his name is inseparably connected with one of the chief instruments of analysis, just as that of Descartes—another philosopher —is with analytical geometry.

233. **The Bernoullis.** Leibnitz was but one amongst several continental writers whose papers in the *Acta Eruditorum* familiarized mathematicians with the use of the differential calculus. The most important of these were James and John Bernoulli. Not only did they take a prominent part in nearly every mathematical question then discussed, but a large number of the leading mathematicians on the continent during the first half of the eighteenth century came directly or indirectly under the influence of one or both of them. The first member of the family who attained distinction in mathematics was James.

234. **James Bernoulli, 1654-1705.** James Bernoulli was born at Bâle; in 1687 he was appointed to a chair of mathematics in the university there; and occupied it until his death.

He was one of the earliest to realize the power of the infinitesimal calculus as an instrument of analysis, and he applied it to several problems, but he did not himself invent any new processes. His most important discoveries were a solution of the problem to find an isochronous curve; a proof that the construction for the catenary which had been given by Leibnitz was correct, and an extension of this to strings of variable density and under a central force; the determination of the form taken by an elastic rod fixed at one end and acted on by a given force at the other; also of a flexible rectangular sheet with two sides fixed horizontally and filled with a heavy liquid; and lastly of a sail filled with wind. In 1696 he offered a reward for the general solution of isoperimetrical figures, *i.e.* the determination of a figure of a given species which should include a maximum area, its perimeter being given : his own solution, published in 1701, is correct as far as it goes. In 1713 he established the fundamental principles of the calculus of probabilities; and in the course of his investigation he defined the numbers known by his name and explained their use.

235. **John Bernoulli, 1667-1748.** John Bernoulli, the brother of James, was born at Bâle. He occupied successively the chairs of mathematics at Groningen and at Bâle, where he succeeded his brother. To all who did not acknowledge his merits in a manner commensurate with his own view of them he behaved most unjustly : as an illustration of his character it may be mentioned that he attempted to substitute for an incorrect solution of his own on the problem of isoperimetrical curves another stolen from his brother James, while he expelled his son Daniel from his house for obtaining a prize from the French Academy which he had hoped to receive himself. After the deaths of Leibnitz and l'Hospital he claimed the merit of some of their discoveries; these claims are now known to be false. He was, however, the most successful teacher of his age, and had

the faculty of inspiring his pupils with almost as passionate a zeal for mathematics as he felt himself. The general adoption on the continent of the differential rather than the fluxional notation was largely due to his influence.

236. The chief discoveries of John Bernoulli were the exponential calculus, the treatment of trigonometry as a branch of analysis, the conditions for a geodesic, the determination of orthogonal trajectories, the solution of the brachistochrone, the statement that a ray of light traversed a path such that $\Sigma\mu ds$ was a minimum, and the enunciation of the principle of virtual work. I believe that he was the first to denote the accelerating effect of gravity by an algebraical sign g, and he thus arrived at the formula $v^2 = 2gh$. The notation ϕx to indicate a function of x was introduced by him in 1718, and displaced the notation X or ξ proposed by him in 1698: but the general adoption of symbols like f, F, ϕ, ψ,..., to represent functions, seems to be mainly due to Euler and Lagrange.

237. **The Development of Analysis on the Continent.** Leaving for a moment the English mathematicians of the first half of the eighteenth century, we come next to a number of continental writers who barely escape mediocrity, but whose writings disseminated the methods and language of analytical geometry and of the differential calculus. The most eminent of them were *l'Hospital*, 1661-1704; *Varignon*, 1654-1722; *Nicole*, 1683-1738; and *de Gua*, 1713-1785. The middle of the eighteenth century is noticeable for the writings of *Clairaut*, *D'Alembert*, *Daniel Bernoulli*, and *Euler*. I postpone for a few pages any detailed mention of Euler (see below, arts. 254, 255).

238. **Clairaut, 1713-1765.** Clairaut was born at Paris. When he was eighteen he wrote on tortuous curves, and gave a demonstration of the fact noted by Newton that all cubic curves were projections of one of five parabolas. Ten years later Clairaut went on a scientific expedition to measure the length of a meridian degree on the earth's

surface, and on his return he published his *Théorie de la figure de la terre*. This is founded on a paper by Maclaurin, where it had been shewn that a mass of homogeneous fluid set in rotation about a line through its centre of mass would, under the mutual attraction of its particles, take the form of a spheroid. This work of Clairaut treated of heterogeneous spheroids, and contains the proof of his formula for the accelerating effect of gravity in a place of latitude l, namely, $g = G\{1 + (\tfrac{5}{2}m - \epsilon)\sin^2 l\}$, where G is the value of equatorial gravity, m the ratio of the centrifugal force to gravity at the equator, and ϵ the ellipticity of a meridian section of the earth. In 1849 Stokes shewed that the same result was true whatever was the interior constitution or density of the earth, provided the surface was a spheroid of equilibrium of small ellipticity.

239. Impressed by the power of geometry as shewn in the writings of Newton and Maclaurin, Clairaut abandoned analysis, and his next work on the moon, published in 1752, is cast in a geometrical form. This contains the explanation of the motion of the apse which had previously puzzled astronomers, and which Clairaut had at first deemed so inexplicable that he was on the point of publishing a new hypothesis as to the law of attraction when it occurred to him to carry the approximation to the third order, and he thereupon found that the result was in accordance with the observations.

240. His growing popularity in society hindered his scientific work. "Engagé," says Bossut, "à des soupers, à des veilles, entraîné par un goût vif pour les femmes, voulant allier le plaisir à ses travaux ordinaires, il perdit le repos, la santé, enfin la vie à l'âge de cinquante-deux ans."

241. **D'Alembert, 1717-1783.** Jean-le-Rond D'Alembert was born at Paris in 1717, and being abandoned by his mother on the steps of the little church of St. Jean-le-Rond, which then nestled under the great porch of

Nôtre Dame, he was taken to the parish commissary, who, following the usual practice in such cases, gave him the Christian name of Jean-le-Rond. He was boarded out by the parish with the wife of a glazier in a small way of business, and received a fairly good education.

242. Nearly all his mathematical works were produced during the years 1743 to 1754. The first of these was his work on dynamics, published in 1743, in which he enunciated the principle known by his name, namely, that the "internal forces of inertia" (*i.e.* the forces which resist acceleration) must be equal and opposite to the forces which produce the acceleration. This may be inferred from Newton's second reading of his third law of motion, but the full consequences had not been realized previously. The application of this principle enables us to obtain the differential equations of motion of any rigid system. In the following year D'Alembert applied this principle to the phenomena of hydromechanics. A few years later he gave the earliest solution of a partial differential equation of the second order. His chief remaining contributions to mathematics were on physical astronomy; especially on the precession of the equinoxes, and on variations in the obliquity of the ecliptic.

243. During the latter part of his life he was mainly occupied with the great French encyclopaedia. For this he wrote the introduction and numerous philosophical and mathematical articles; the best are those on geometry and on probabilities. His style is brilliant, but not polished, and faithfully reflects his character, which was bold, honest, and frank. He defended a severe criticism which he had offered on some mediocre work by the remark, "j'aime mieux être incivil qu'ennuyé," and with his dislike of sycophants and bores, it is not surprising that during his life he had more enemies than friends. It is to his credit that he refused to leave his adopted mother, with whom he continued to live until her death in 1757.

It cannot be said that she sympathized with his success, for at the height of his fame she remonstrated with him for wasting his talents on such work. "Vous ne serez jamais qu'un philosophe," said she, "et qu'est-ce qu'un philosophe ? c'est un fou qui se tourmente pendant sa vie, pour qu'on parle de lui lorsqu'il n'y sera plus."

244. **Daniel Bernoulli, 1700-1782.** Daniel Bernoulli, who was the ablest of the younger Bernoullis, was a contemporary and intimate friend of Euler, whose works are mentioned below. He went to St. Petersburg in 1724 as professor of mathematics, but the roughness of the social life was distasteful to him, and he was not sorry when a temporary illness in 1733 allowed him to plead his health as an excuse for leaving. He then returned to Bâle, and held successively chairs of medicine, metaphysics, and natural philosophy there.

245. His earliest mathematical work, published in 1724, contains a theory of the oscillations of rigid bodies, and a solution of the differential equation proposed by Riccati. Two years later he pointed out the advantage of resolving a compound motion into separate motions of translation and motions of rotation. His chief work is his *Hydrodynamique*, published in 1738. It resembles Lagrange's work on mechanics in being arranged so that all the results are consequences of a single principle, namely, in this case, the conservation of energy. This was followed by a memoir on the theory of the tides, to which, conjointly with memoirs by Euler and Maclaurin, a prize was awarded by the French Academy. These three memoirs contain all that was done on this subject between the publication of Newton's *Principia* and the investigations of Laplace. Bernoulli also wrote a large number of papers on various mechanical questions, especially on problems connected with vibrating strings, and the solutions thereof given by Taylor and by D'Alembert. He is the earliest writer who attempted to formulate a kinetic

theory of gases, and he applied the idea to explain the law associated with the names of Boyle and Mariotte.

246. British Mathematicians of the Eighteenth Century. It was natural that the English should at first have adopted the notation of Newton in the infinitesimal calculus in preference to that of Leibnitz. Their adherence to that notation was mainly due to the just resentment felt at the action of Leibnitz and John Bernoulli, but the effect was unfortunate, as it tended to isolate them from their continental contemporaries. The leading members of the English school were *Halley*, 1656-1742 ; *Taylor*, 1685-1731 ; *Cotes*, 1682-1716, who made the earliest attempt to frame a theory of errors ; *Demoivre*, 1667-1754, who created a part of trigonometry dealing with imaginary quantities, and wrote on recurring series and on partial fractions ; *Maclaurin*, 1698-1746 ; and *Thomas Simpson*, 1710-1761. Here I can only spare space to mention briefly the researches of Taylor and Maclaurin.

247. Taylor, 1685-1731. Brook Taylor, educated at Cambridge, was among the most enthusiastic of Newton's admirers. His earliest work, published in 1715, contains a proof of the well-known theorem

$$f(x+h) = f(x) + hf'(x) + \tfrac{1}{2}h^2 f''(x) + \ldots,$$

by which a function of a single variable can be expanded in powers of it. Among other applications of the calculus he gave the theory of the transverse vibrations of strings. He determined the differential equation of the path of a ray of light when traversing a heterogeneous medium ; and, assuming that the density of the air depends only on its distance from the earth's surface, obtained by means of quadratures the approximate form of the curve. He also discussed the form of the catenary and the determination of the centres of oscillation and percussion. His treatise on perspective, published in 1719, contains the earliest general enunciation of the principle of vanishing points.

248. **Maclaurin, 1698-1746.** Colin Maclaurin, born in Argyllshire, occupied successively chairs of mathematics at Aberdeen and at Edinburgh. In 1745 he took an active part in opposing the advance of the Young Pretender: on the approach of the Highlanders he fled to York, but the exposure in the trenches at Edinburgh and the privations he endured in his escape proved fatal to him.

249. His *Geometria Organica*, 1719, is on the extension of a theorem given by Newton. Newton had shewn that, if two angles bounded by straight lines turn round their respective summits so that the point of intersection of two of these lines moves along a straight line, the other point of intersection will describe a conic; and, if the first point move along a conic, the second will describe a quartic. Maclaurin gave an analytical discussion of the general theorem, and shewed how by this method various curves could be practically traced. This work contains an elaborate discussion on curves and their pedals. In the following year Maclaurin issued a supplement on diameters, asymptotes, and various geometrical theorems.

250. His work on fluxions, published in 1742, contained a systematic exposition of the method. In it he gave a proof of the theorem that

$$f(x) = f(0) + xf'(0) + \tfrac{1}{2}x^2 f''(0) + \dots .$$

The result had been given in 1730 by James Stirling, and of course is at once deducible from Taylor's theorem, on which the proofs by Stirling and Maclaurin are admittedly founded. Maclaurin also here enunciated the important theorem that, if $\phi(x)$ be positive and decrease as x increases from $x = a$ to $x = \infty$, then the series

$$\phi(a) + \phi(a+1) + \phi(a+2) + \dots$$

is convergent or divergent as $\int_a^\infty \phi(x)\, dx$ is finite or infinite.

He also gave the correct theory of maxima and minima, and rules for finding and discriminating multiple points.

251. This treatise is, however, especially valuable for the solutions it contains of numerous problems in geometry, statics, the theory of attractions, and astronomy. To solve these he reverted to classical methods, and so powerful did these processes seem, when used by him, that Clairaut after reading the work abandoned analysis, and attacked the problem of the figure of the earth again by pure geometry. At a later time this part of the book was described by Lagrange as the "chef d'œuvre de géométrie qu'on peut comparer à tout ce qu'Archimède nous a laissé de plus beau et de plus ingénieux." Maclaurin here determined the attraction of a homogeneous ellipsoid at an internal point, and gave some theorems on its attraction at an external point; in effecting this he introduced the conception of level surfaces, *i.e.* surfaces at every point of which the resultant attraction is perpendicular to the surface. No further advance in the theory of attractions was made until Lagrange in 1773 introduced the idea of the potential. Maclaurin also shewed that a spheroid was a possible form of equilibrium of a mass of homogeneous liquid rotating about an axis passing through its centre of mass. Finally he discussed the theory of the tides.

252. **Decay of the British School.** In the early years of the eighteenth century the English school appeared vigorous and fruitful, but decadence rapidly set in, and after the deaths of Maclaurin and Simpson no British mathematician appeared who is fairly comparable to the continental mathematicians of the latter half of the eighteenth century. This fact is partly explicable by the isolation of the school, partly by its tendency to rely too exclusively on geometrical and fluxional methods. Some attention was however given to practical science, but it was not until about 1820, when analytical methods came into vogue, that English mathematics again became interesting.

253. Development of the Continental School. On the continent, under the influence of John Bernoulli, the calculus had, by the middle of the eighteenth century, become an instrument of great analytical power expressed in an admirable notation—and for practical applications it is impossible to over-estimate the value of a good notation. The subject of mechanics remained, however, in much the condition in which Newton had left it, until D'Alembert, by making use of the differential calculus, did something to extend it. Universal gravitation as enunciated in the *Principia* was accepted as an established fact, but the geometrical methods adopted in proving it were difficult to follow or to use in analogous problems; Maclaurin, Simpson, and Clairaut may be regarded as the last mathematicians of distinction who employed them.

·The leading mathematicians of the era on which we are now entering are Euler, Lagrange, Laplace, and Legendre. Briefly we may say that Euler extended, summed up, and completed the work of his predecessors; while Lagrange, with almost unrivalled skill, developed the infinitesimal calculus and theoretical mechanics, and reduced them to the forms with which we are familiar. At the same time Laplace made some additions to the infinitesimal calculus, and applied that calculus to the theory of universal gravitation; he also created a calculus of probabilities. Legendre invented spherical harmonic analysis, called attention to elliptic integrals, and added to the theory of numbers.

254. Euler, 1707-1783. Euler was the son of a Lutheran minister at Bâle, and was educated in his native town under John Bernoulli. He settled in Russia as professor, but the severity of the climate affected his eyesight, and in 1735 he completely lost the use of one eye. In 1741 he moved to Berlin at the request, or rather command, of Frederick the Great; here he stayed till 1766, when he returned to Russia, and was succeeded at Berlin by Lagrange. Within two or three years of his going back to St. Petersburg he became blind; but in spite of this, and although his house together with many of his papers were burnt in 1771, he continued his labours and recast many of his earlier papers and books.

255. I think we may sum up Euler's work by saying that he greatly extended the methods of analysis, and revised almost all the branches of pure mathematics which were then known, filling up the details, adding proofs, and arranging the whole in a consistent form. Such work is very important, and it is fortunate for science when it falls into hands as competent as those of Euler. Besides his classical researches on algebra (determinate and indeterminate), trigonometry, analytical geometry, and the calculus (including the earliest use of the calculus of variations), he wrote on mechanics, physics, and astronomy.

256. Of course Euler's magnificent works were not the only text-books containing original matter produced at this time. Amongst numerous writers other than those mentioned above, I would specially single out the name of *Lambert*, 1728-1777, a distinguished Prussian mathematician. But as we approach modern times the number of capable and even brilliant mathematicians becomes so large that I am obliged to confine myself to mentioning only those of exceptional genius. I therefore proceed at once to describe the works of Lagrange.

257. **Lagrange, 1736-1813.** Lagrange, the greatest mathematician of the eighteenth century, was born at Turin. His father, who had the charge of the Sardinian military chest, was of good social position and wealthy; but before his son grew up had lost most of his property in speculations, and young Lagrange had to rely for his position on his own abilities. He was educated at Turin, but he shewed no taste for mathematics until he was seventeen, when he took up the study unaided. The first fruit of these labours was his letter, written when

he was still only nineteen, to Euler, in which he solved the isoperimetrical problem which for more than half a century had been a subject of discussion. To effect the solution (in which he sought to determine the form of a function so that a formula in which it entered should satisfy a certain condition) he enunciated the principles of the calculus of variations. Euler recognized the generality of the method adopted, and its superiority to that used by himself; and with rare courtesy he withheld a paper he had previously written, which covered some of the same ground, in order that the young Italian might have time to complete his work, and claim the undisputed invention of the new calculus.

258. The last-mentioned memoir placed Lagrange in the front rank of mathematicians. Five years later he stood without a rival as the foremost mathematician living; but the unceasing labour of the preceding years had seriously affected his health, and the doctors refused to be responsible for his reason or life unless he would take rest and exercise. Although his health was temporarily restored his nervous system never quite recovered its tone, and henceforth he constantly suffered from attacks of profound melancholy.

259. In 1764 he left Italy to visit London, but on the way fell ill at Paris. There he was received with the most marked honour, and it was with regret he left the brilliant society of that city to return to his provincial life at Turin. His further stay in Piedmont was, however, short. In 1766 Euler left Berlin, and Frederick the Great immediately wrote expressing the wish of "the greatest king in Europe" to have "the greatest mathematician in Europe" resident at his court. Lagrange accepted the offer, and spent the next twenty years in Prussia.

260. His mental activity during these years at Berlin was amazing. Not only did he produce his splendid *Mécanique analytique*, but he contributed between one and two hundred papers to various Academies. Some of these

H

are complete treatises, and all without exception are of a high order of excellence. They include the solution of many most difficult problems in algebra, in the theory of numbers, in differential equations (which he put on a scientific basis), in finite differences, in the theory of attractions (wherein he introduced in 1773 the idea of the potential), and in astronomy.

261. Over and above these various papers, he composed his great treatise, the *Mécanique analytique*. In this he laid down the law of virtual work, and from that fundamental principle, by the aid of the calculus of variations, deduced the whole of mechanics, both of solids and fluids. The method of generalized coordinates, by means of which he gave general formulae from which any particular result can be obtained, is perhaps the most brilliant result of his analysis. Instead of following the motion of each individual part of a material system, as Newton, D'Alembert, and Euler had done, he shewed that, if we determine its configuration by a sufficient number of variables whose number is the same as that of the degrees of freedom possessed by the system, then the kinetic and potential energies of the system can be expressed in terms of these variables, and the differential equations of motion thence deduced by mere differentiation.

262. In 1787 Frederick died, and Lagrange, who had found the climate of Berlin trying, gladly accepted the offer of Louis XVI. to migrate to Paris. He received similar invitations from Spain and Naples. In France he was received with every mark of distinction, and special apartments in the Louvre were prepared for his reception. At the beginning of his residence here he was seized with an attack of melancholy, and even the printed copy of his *Mécanique* on which he had worked for a quarter of a century lay for more than two years unopened on his desk. Curiosity as to the results of the French Revolution first stirred him out of his lethargy, a curiosity which soon

turned to alarm as the revolution developed. It was about the same time, 1792, that the unaccountable sadness of his life and his timidity moved the compassion of a young girl who insisted on marrying him, and proved a devoted wife to whom he became warmly attached. Although the decree of October, 1793, which ordered all foreigners to leave France, specially exempted him by name, he was preparing to escape when he was offered the presidency of the commission for the reform of weights and measures. It is largely to his influence that we owe the choice of the units finally selected and their decimal subdivision.

Though Lagrange had determined to escape from France while there was yet time, he was never in any danger; and the different revolutionary governments (and at a later time Napoleon) paid him marked distinction. A striking testimony to the respect in which he was held was shewn in 1796, when the French commissary in Italy was ordered to attend in state on Lagrange's father, and tender the congratulations of the republic on the achievements of his son, who "had done honour to all mankind by his genius, and whom it was the special glory of Piedmont to have produced."

263. In appearance Lagrange was of medium height, and slightly formed, with pale blue eyes, and a colourless complexion. In character he was nervous and timid, he detested controversy, and to avoid it willingly allowed others to take the credit of what he had himself done. His interests were essentially those of a student of pure mathematics: he sought and obtained far-reaching abstract results, and was content to leave the applications to others. Indeed no inconsiderable part of the discoveries of his great contemporary Laplace consisted of the application of the Lagrangian formulae to the facts of nature; for example, Laplace's conclusions on the velocity of sound and the secular acceleration of the moon are implicitly involved in Lagrange's results.

264. **Laplace, 1749-1827.** Laplace was the son of a small cottager, or perhaps a farm labourer, in Normandy, and owed his education to the interest excited in some wealthy neighbours by his abilities and engaging presence. Very little is known of his early years, for when he became distinguished he held himself aloof both from his relatives and from those who had assisted him. A similar pettiness of character marked many of his actions. It would seem that about 1770 he obtained a mastership in a military school, and that then, being secure of a competency, he threw himself into original research. Later, he became professor at Paris, and continued to occupy various official positions until his death.

265. During the years 1784-1787 he produced some memoirs of exceptional power. Prominent among these is one in which he completely determined the attraction of a spheroid on a particle outside it : this is memorable for the introduction into analysis of spherical harmonics or Laplace's coefficients, and for the development of the use of the potential. This memoir was followed by another on planetary inequalities, wherein it was shewn by general considerations that the mutual action of two planets could never largely affect the eccentricities and inclinations of their orbits. Finally, in 1787, Laplace gave the explanation of the relation between the lunar acceleration and the secular changes in the eccentricity of the earth's orbit : this investigation completed the proof of the stability of the solar system on the assumption that it consists of a collection of rigid bodies.

266. Laplace now set himself the task to write a work which should "offer a complete solution of the great mechanical problem presented by the solar system, and bring theory to coincide so closely with observation that empirical equations should no longer find a place in astronomical tables." The result is embodied in the *Exposition du système du monde* and the *Mécanique céleste.* The

former was published in 1796, and gives a general explanation of the phenomena with a summary of the history
of astronomy, but omits all details. The latter contains
a full analytical discussion of the subject. The first
two volumes contain methods for calculating the motions
of the planets, determining their figures, and resolving tidal problems. The third and fourth volumes
contain the application of these methods, and also several
astronomical tables. The fifth and last volume is mainly
historical, but it gives as appendices the results of Laplace's
latest researches. This work is more than the translation
of the *Principia* into the language of the differential
calculus, for it completes parts of which Newton had
been unable to fill in the details.

267. Laplace went in state to beg Napoleon to accept a
copy of his work, and the following account of the inter-
view is well authenticated, and so characteristic of all
the parties concerned that I quote it in full. Someone
had told Napoleon that the book contained no mention of
the name of God; Napoleon, who was fond of putting
embarrassing questions, received it with the remark,
" M. Laplace, they tell me you have written this large book
on the system of the universe, and have never even mentioned its Creator." Laplace, who, though the most supple
of politicians, was rigid on every point of his philosophy,
drew himself up and answered bluntly, "Je n'avais pas
besoin de cette hypothèse-là." Napoleon, greatly amused,
told this reply to Lagrange, who exclaimed, "Ah! c'est
une belle hypothèse; ça explique beaucoup de choses."

268. In 1812 Laplace issued his work on probabilities.
This treatise includes an exposition of the method of
least squares, which is a remarkable illustration of Laplace's
command over the processes of analysis. The method of
least squares for the combination of numerous observa
tions had been given empirically by Gauss and Legendre,
but the fourth chapter of this work contains a formal proof

of it, on which the theory of errors has been since based.

269. Laplace seems to have regarded analysis merely as a means of attacking physical problems, though the ability with which he invented the necessary analysis is almost phenomenal. As long as his results were true he took but little trouble to explain the steps by which he arrived at them; he never studied elegance or symmetry in his processes, and it was sufficient for him if he could by any means solve the particular question he was discussing.

270. It would have been well for Laplace's reputation had he been content with his scientific work, but above all things he coveted social fame. The skill and rapidity with which he changed his politics as occasion required would be amusing had they not been so servile. As Napoleon's power increased Laplace abandoned his republican principles, and begged the first consul to give him the post of minister of the interior. Napoleon, who desired the support of men of science, accepted the offer; but a little less than six weeks saw the close of Laplace's political career. Napoleon's memorandum on the subject is as follows: "Géomètre de premier rang, Laplace ne tarda pas à se montrer administrateur plus que médiocre; dès son premier travail nous reconnûmes que nous nous étions trompé. Laplace ne saisissait aucune question sous son véritable point de vue: il cherchait des subtilités partout, n'avait que des idées problématiques, et portait enfin l'esprit des 'infiniment petits' jusque dans l'administration."

Although Laplace was expelled from office it was desirable to retain his allegiance. He was accordingly raised to the senate, and to the third volume of the *Mécanique céleste* he prefixed a note that of all the truths therein contained the most precious to the author was the declaration he thus made of his devotion towards the peace-maker of Europe. In copies sold after the restoration this was struck out. In 1814 it was evident that the empire was falling; Laplace hastened to tender his services to the Bourbons, and on the restoration was rewarded with the title of marquis. His knowledge was useful on the numerous scientific commissions on which he served, and probably accounts for the manner in which his political insincerity was overlooked.

271. That Laplace was vain and selfish is not denied by his warmest admirers; his conduct to the benefactors of his youth and his political friends was contemptible; while his appropriation of the results of those who were comparatively unknown seems to be well established —of these, three subsequently rose to distinction (Legendre and Fourier in France and Young in England), and never forgot the injustice of which they had been the victims. On the other side it may be said that on some questions he shewed independence of character, and he never concealed his views on religion, philosophy, or science however diatasteful they might be to the authorities in power; it should be also added that towards the close of his life and especially to the work of his pupils Laplace was both generous and appreciative, and in one case suppressed a paper of his own in order that a pupil might have the sole credit of the investigation.

272. **Legendre, 1752-1833.** Legendre, born at Toulouse, was educated in Paris. He held a few minor government appointments, but the influence of Laplace was steadily exerted against his obtaining office or public recognition, and Legendre, who was a timid student, accepted the obscurity to which the hostility of his colleague condemned him.

273. Legendre's analysis is of a high order of excellence, and is second only to that produced by Lagrange and Laplace, though it is not so original. His memoirs on attractions, his use of circular (or zonal) harmonics and of the potential, and his papers on geodesy and on the

method of least squares are specially noticeable. In his theory of numbers he carried the subject as far as was possible by the application of ordinary algebra, but he did not realize that it might be regarded as a higher arithmetic, and so form a distinct subject in mathematics. His work on the integral calculus includes some account of integration by series, definite integrals, and in particular an elaborate discussion of the Beta and the Gamma functions. He treated the theory of elliptic integrals merely as a problem in the integral calculus, but did not see that it might be considered as a higher trigonometry, and so constitute a distinct branch of analysis. The modern treatment is founded on that introduced by Abel and Jacobi: the superiority of their methods was at once recognized by Legendre, and almost the last act of his life was to recommend those discoveries which he knew would consign his own labours to comparative oblivion.

274. **The Creation of Modern Geometry.** While Euler, Lagrange, Laplace, and Legendre were perfecting analysis, the members of another group of French mathematicians were extending the range of geometry by methods similar to those previously used by Desargues and Pascal. The most eminent of those who created modern synthetic geometry was Poncelet (1788-1867), but the subject is also associated with the names of Monge (1746-1818) and L. Carnot (1753-1823). Its development in more recent times is largely due to Steiner, von Staudt, and Cremona (see below, arts. 315, 316).

275. **The Development of Mathematical Physics.** It will be noticed that Lagrange, Laplace, and Legendre mostly occupied themselves with analysis, geometry, higher arithmetic, and astronomy. The later members of the French school devoted themselves largely to the application of mathematical analysis to physics. Before considering these mathematicians, I may mention the names of two distinguished English experimental physicists—

Henry Cavendish (1731-1810) and Thomas Young (1773-1829)—of whose work their French contemporaries made some use.

276. **Fourier, 1768-1830.** Fourier took a prominent part in his own district in promoting the revolution, and was rewarded by an appointment in 1795 in the Normal school, and subsequently by a chair at the Polytechnic school. In 1822 he published his work on the analytical theory of heat, in which he based his reasoning on Newton's law of cooling, namely, that the flow of heat between two adjacent molecules is proportional to the infinitely small difference of their temperatures. In this work he shewed that any function of a variable, whether continuous or discontinuous, can be expanded in a series of sines of multiples of the variable; a result which is constantly used in modern analysis.

277. **Poisson, 1781-1840.** Poisson is almost equally distinguished for his applications of mathematics to mechanics and to physics. His father had been a common soldier, and on his retirement was given a small administrative post in his native village: when the revolution broke out he appears to have assumed the government of the place, and, being left undisturbed, became a person of some local importance. The boy was put out to nurse, and he used to tell how one day his father, coming to see him, found that the nurse had gone out on pleasure bent, while she had left him suspended by a small cord to a nail fixed in the wall. This she explained was a necessary precaution to prevent him from perishing under the teeth of the various animals and insects that roamed on the floor. Poisson used to add that his gymnastic efforts carried him incessantly from one side to the other, and it was thus in his tenderest infancy that he commenced those studies on the pendulum that were to occupy so large a part of his mature age.

278. At the age of seventeen he entered the Polytechnic,

and his abilities excited the interest of Lagrange and Laplace, whose friendship he retained to the end of their lives. A memoir on finite differences, which he wrote when only eighteen, was reported on so favourably by Legendre that it was ordered to be printed. As soon as he had finished his course he was made a lecturer at the school, and he continued through his life to hold various government scientific posts and professorships. He was somewhat of a socialist, and remained a rigid republican till 1815, when, with a view to making another empire impossible, he joined the legitimists. He took, however, no active part in politics, and made the study of mathematics his amusement as well as his business.

279. Of his memoirs on the subject of pure mathematics the most important are those on definite integrals and Fourier's series, their application to physical problems constituting one of his chief claims to distinction; his essay on the calculus of variations; and his papers on the probability of the mean results of observations. Of his memoirs in applied mathematics, perhaps the most remarkable are those on the theory of electrostatics and magnetism, which originated a new branch of mathematical physics : he supposed that the results were due to the attractions and repulsions of imponderable particles. The most important of those on physical astronomy are the two on the secular inequalities of the mean motions of the planets, and on the variation of arbitrary constants introduced into the solutions of questions on mechanics ; in these Poisson discussed the question of the stability of the planetary orbits (which Lagrange had already established to the first degree of approximation for the disturbing forces), and shewed that the result can be extended to the third order of small quantities.

280. **The French School, circ. 1830.** A period of exceptional intellectual activity in any school or subject is usually followed by one of comparative stagnation ;

and after the deaths of Lagrange, Laplace, Legendre, and Poisson, the French school, which had occupied so prominent a position at the beginning of this century, ceased for some years (except for Cauchy, who is mentioned below) to produce much new work.

281. **The Introduction of Analysis into England.** The isolation of the English school and its devotion to geometrical methods are the most marked features in its history during the latter half of the eighteenth century; and the absence of any considerable and valuable contribution to the advancement of mathematical science was a natural consequence.   Towards the close of the last century the more thoughtful Cambridge mathematicians began to recognize that their isolation from their continental contemporaries was a serious evil.   The earliest attempt in England to popularize the notation and methods of the calculus as used on the continent was due to Woodhouse (1773-1827).   It is doubtful if he could have brought the analytical methods into vogue by himself; but his views were enthusiastically adopted by three younger men, Babbage, Peacock, and John Herschel, who succeeded in carrying out the reforms he had suggested.

In 1817, and again in 1819, the differential notation was employed in the university examinations, and after 1820 its use was well established.   This was followed by the issue in 1820 of two volumes of examples illustrative of the new method; one by Peacock on the differential and integral calculus, and the other by Herschel on the calculus of finite differences.   These efforts were supplemented by the rapid publication of good text-books in which analysis was freely used.   The employment of analytical methods spread from Cambridge over the rest of Britain, and by 1830 had come into general use.

Recent Mathematics.

282. Commencement of a New Era. The mathematics of the nineteenth century may be said to commence a new era, marked partly by an immense extension of the subjects of pure mathematics (such as the theory of numbers; higher algebra, including the theory of forms; the theory of equations; the creation of a theory of functions, including those of double and multiple periodicity; and higher geometry), and partly by the inclusion of many branches of physics within the scope of mathematics. Much of this is too technical for popular exposition; and, even were it otherwise, the remainder of this primer would be necessarily written at a disadvantage, since it is only in rare cases that I have allowed myself to allude here to the works of mathematicians still living.

283. Rise of Modern German Mathematical Schools. While the French school, which distinguished the close of the last century, was entering on a period of temporary inactivity, and the British school was only awaking to the importance of making a more extended use of analysis, a new German school had already arisen, which has affected most profoundly the mathematics of the present century. At the same time it must be remembered that the different nations of the western world are now related so intimately that the schools of modern countries and times are not separated by rigid barriers.

The works of no mathematician of this century have had a wider influence on his contemporaries than those of Gauss, and I proceed to describe briefly his more important researches.

284. Gauss, 1777-1855. Gauss was born at Brunswick; his father was a bricklayer, and he was indebted for a liberal education (much against the will of his

parents, who wished to profit by his wages as a labourer)
to the notice which his talents procured from the reigning
duke. In 1792 he was sent to the Caroline College, and
by 1795 professors and pupils alike admitted that he knew
all that the former could teach him : it was while there
that he investigated the method of least squares, and
proved by induction the law of quadratic reciprocity.
Thence he went to Göttingen, where he studied under
Kästner : many of his discoveries in the theory of numbers were made while a student here. In 1798 he returned
to Brunswick, where he earned a somewhat precarious
livelihood by private tuition.

285. In 1799 Gauss published his demonstration that
every algebraical equation has a root ; a theorem of which
altogether he gave three distinct proofs. In 1801 this was
followed by his *Disquisitiones Arithmeticae* described below.
His next discovery was in a totally different department
of mathematics. The absence of a planet in the space
between Mars and Jupiter, where Bode's law would have
led observers to expect one, had been long remarked, but
it was not till 1801 that any one of the numerous group of
minor planets which occupy that space was observed. The
discovery was made under conditions which appeared
to render it impracticable to forecast the orbit of the
planet. Fortunately the observations were communicated
to Gauss; he calculated its elements, and his analysis
proved him to be the first of theoretical astronomers no
less than the greatest of "arithmeticians."

The attention excited by these investigations procured
for him in 1807 the offer of a chair at St. Petersburg, which
he declined. In the same year he was appointed director
of the Göttingen Observatory and professor of astronomy
there : these offices he retained to his death. For some
years after 1807 his time was mainly occupied by work
connected with his observatory } but in 1809 he published
a treatise which contributed largely to the improvement

of practical astronomy and introduced the principle of curvilinear triangulation.

286. His researches on electricity and magnetism date from about the year 1830. Two memoirs on these subjects may be specially mentioned, one on the general theory of earth-magnetism, and the other on the theory of forces attracting according to the inverse square of the distance. Like Poisson he treated the phenomena in electrostatics as due to attractions and repulsions between imponderable particles. In electrodynamics he discovered (in 1835) that the attraction between two electrified particles depends on their relative motion and position according to Weber's well known formula; but as he could not devise any reasonably probable physical hypothesis from which he could deduce the result, he abandoned the subject. His researches on optics, and especially on systems of lenses, were published in 1840. I will now mention very briefly some of the most important of his discoveries in pure mathematics.

287. His most celebrated work in pure mathematics is the *Disquisitiones Arithmeticae*. This treatise and Legendre's work remain authorities on the theory of numbers; but, just as in his discussion of elliptic functions, Legendre failed to rise to the conception of a new subject, and confined himself to regarding their theory as a chapter in the integral calculus, so he treated the theory of numbers as a chapter in algebra. Gauss, however, realized that the theory of discrete magnitudes or higher arithmetic was of a different kind from that of continuous magnitudes or algebra, and he introduced a new notation and new methods of analysis, of which subsequent writers have generally availed themselves.

288. The theory of numbers may be divided into two main divisions, namely, the theory of forms and the theory of congruences. The solution of the problem of the representation of numbers by binary quadratic forms is due to Gauss; he added some results relating to ternary

quadratic forms, involving two indeterminates, but the general extension from two to three indeterminates was the work of Eisenstein (see below, art. 294). Gauss also discussed the question of biquadratic residues (wherein the notion of complex numbers of the form $a + bi$ was introduced into the theory of numbers). Moreover, he invented the theory of congruences of the first and second orders. He also discussed the solution of binomial equations of the form $x^n = 1$: this involves the celebrated theorem that the only regular polygons which can be constructed by elementary geometry are those of which the number of sides is $2^m(2^n + 1)$, where m and n are integers and $2^n + 1$ is a prime.

289. The modern theory of functions of double periodicity has its origin in the discoveries of Abel and Jacobi, both of whom arrived at the theta functions. Gauss, however, had independently, and at an earlier date (1808), discovered these functions and their chief properties; having been led to them by certain integrals, to evaluate which he invented the transformation now associated with the name of Jacobi.

290. Of Gauss's remaining memoirs in pure mathematics the most remarkable are those on the theory of determinants; that relating to the proof of the theorem that every numerical equation has a real or imaginary root; that on the summation of series; that on hypergeometric series, which contains a discussion of the Gamma function; and lastly, one on interpolation: his introduction of rigorous tests for the convergency of infinite series is specially noticeable. We have also the important memoir on the conformal representation of one surface upon another, in which the results given by Lagrange for surfaces of revolution are generalized for all surfaces. Finally, in the theory of attractions we have a paper on the attraction of homogeneous ellipsoids; and a memoir wherein it is shewn that the secular variations, which the elements of the orbit of a planet experience from the attraction of a disturbing

planet, are the same as if the mass of the disturbing planet were distributed over its orbit into an elliptic ring in such a manner that equal masses of the ring would correspond to arcs of the orbit described in equal times.

291. From this sketch it will be seen that the ground covered by Gauss's researches was extraordinarily wide, and it may be added that in many cases these researches served to initiate new lines of work. He was, however, the last of the great mathematicians whose interests were nearly universal. Since his time the literature of most branches of mathematics has grown so fast that mathematicians have been forced to specialize in some particular depart- ment or departments.

292. **Comparison of the styles of Lagrange, La- place, and Gauss.** The great masters of modern analysis are Lagrange, Laplace, and Gauss, who were contemporaries. It is interesting to note the marked contrast in their styles. Lagrange was perfect both in form and matter, he was careful to explain his procedure, and, though his arguments are general, they are easy to follow. Laplace on the other hand explained nothing, was absolutely indifferent to style, and, if satisfied that his results were correct, was content to leave them either with no proof or even with a faulty one. Gauss was as exact and elegant as Lagrange, but even more difficult to follow than Laplace, for he removed every trace of the analysis by which he reached his results, and studied to give a proof which, while rigorous, should be as concise and synthetical as possible.

293. The researches of Gauss on the *Theory of Numbers* were continued or supplemented by various mathema- ticians : notably by Lejeune Dirichlet of Göttingen (1805- 1859), Riemann of Göttingen (1826-1866), and Tchebycheff of St. Petersburg (1821-1894), who discussed in particu- lar the distribution of primes (see below art. 302); by Jacobi of Berlin, who wrote on residues (see below art. 300); and by Eisenstein of Berlin and Henry Smith of Oxford,

whose researches on the theory of forms I proceed briefly to indicate.

294. **Eisenstein, 1823-1852.** The theory of ternary quadratic forms is due to Eisenstein. He also considered the theorems relating to the possibility of representing a number as a sum of squares, and shewed that the general theorem was limited to eight squares. The cases in which the number of squares is uneven involve some difficulty : Eisenstein gave the solution in the case of three squares, he also left a statement of the solution he had obtained in the case of five squares. Among his other investigations I may mention the remarkable rule he enunciated, by means of which it is possible to distinguish whether a given series represents an algebraical or a transcendental function.

295. **Henry Smith, 1826-1883.** One of the most original and powerful mathematicians of modern writers on the theory of numbers was Henry Smith. He was educated at Rugby and Oxford; in 1861 he was elected Savilian professor of geometry at Oxford, and resided there till his death. The special subject in connection with which Smith's name will be always associated is his work on linear indeterminate equations and congruences, and on the orders and genera of ternary quadratic forms. He gave demonstrations of Eisenstein's results, their extension to ternary quadratic forms of an even determinant, and a complete classification of ternary quadratic forms : moreover, he did not confine himself to the case of three indeterminates, but succeeded in establishing the principles on which the case of n indeterminates depends, and obtained the general formulae.

296. *The Theory of Functions of Double and Multiple Periodicity* is another subject to which much attention has been paid during this century. I have already mentioned that Gauss discovered the theta functions and their chief properties, but his investigations remained for many years concealed in his note-books; and it was to the researches

made between 1820 and 1830 by Abel and Jacobi that
the modern development of the subject is due.   Their
treatment of it has completely superseded that used by
Legendre, and they are justly reckoned as the creators
of this branch of mathematics.

297. **Abel, 1802-1829.**   Abel was born in Norway,
and died at Arendal at the age of twenty-six.   His
memoirs on elliptic functions treat the subject from the
point of view of the theory of equations and algebraic
forms, a treatment to which his researches naturally led
him.   The important result known as Abel's theorem,
which was subsequently applied by Riemann to the theory
of transcendental functions, was written in 1828; the
name of Abelian function has been given to the higher
transcendents of multiple periodicity which were first discussed by Abel.   As illustrating his fertility of ideas, I
may in passing notice his celebrated demonstration that
it is impossible to solve a quintic equation by means of
radicals.

298. **Jacobi, 1804-1851.**   Jacobi, born of Jewish parents
at Potsdam, was educated at the university of Berlin.
In 1827 he became professor at Königsberg; in 1842 the
Prussian Government gave him a pension, and he then
moved to Berlin, where he continued to live till his
death.

299. Jacobi's most celebrated investigations are those on
elliptic functions, the modern notation in which is due to
him, and the theory of which he established simultaneously
with Abel, but independently of him.   Jacobi, like Abel,
recognized that elliptic functions were not merely a group
of theorems on integration, but that they were types of
a new kind of function, namely, one of double periodicity;
hence the particular attention which he paid to the theta
function.   We may say that he commenced the discussion
by considering singly infinite products, while Abel began
by considering doubly infinite products.

300. Among Jacobi's other investigations I may single
out his papers on determinants, and his invention of the
Jacobian, that is, of the functional determinant formed
by the n^2 partial differential coefficients of the first order
of n given functions of n independent variables. I may
also mention his papers on Abelian transcendents; his
investigations on the theory of numbers, wherein he first
proved the law of cubic reciprocity, discussed the theory of
residues, and gave a table of residues of prime roots; his
important work on the theory of partial differential equations; his development of the calculus of variations; and his
numerous memoirs on the planetary theory and other
particular dynamical problems, in the course of which he
extended the theory of differential equations.

301. **Riemann, 1826-1866.** Riemann, one of the most
original and powerful mathematicians of this century, was
born in Hanover, studied at Göttingen under Gauss, and
subsequently at Berlin under Jacobi, Dirichlet, Steiner,
and Eisenstein, all of whom were professors there at
the same time. He subsequently occupied a chair at
Göttingen.

302. Riemann's earliest paper, written in 1850, was on
algebraic functions of a complex variable. In 1854 he wrote
his celebrated memoir on the hypotheses on which geometry
is founded. This was succeeded by memoirs on the theory
of numbers and elliptic functions. In multiply periodic
functions it is hardly too much to say that he did for
the Abelian functions what Abel had done for the elliptic
functions, and it is this perhaps that constitutes his chief
claim to distinction. In the theory of numbers he discussed the number of primes which lie between two
given numbers. Legendre had previously shewn that the
number of primes less than n is very approximately
$n/(\log_e n - 1\cdot08366)$; but Riemann went further, and this
tract and a memoir by Tchebycheff contain nearly all
that has been done yet in connection with a problem

which must have suggested itself to nearly every writer on the subject.

303. **Weierstrass.** While mentioning the theta functions, I ought to allude to the work of Weierstrass, who is now professor in Berlin. In his earlier researches he treated them under a modified form, in which they are expressible in powers of the modulus. At a later period he developed a method for treating all elliptic functions in a symmetrical manner. This has extended and revolutionized the treatment of the subject; in this theory the theta functions are independent of the form of their space boundaries.

304. The consideration of algebraical, trigonometrical, elliptic, hyperelliptic, and other special kinds of functions paved the way for a *Theory of Functions*, which promises to prove a most important and far-reaching branch of mathematics. To a large extent this is the work of living mathematicians, and therefore outside the limits of this primer.

305. The theory of numbers may be considered as a higher arithmetic, and the theory of elliptic and Abelian functions as a higher trigonometry. The *Theory of Higher Algebra* (including the *Theory of Equations*) has also attracted considerable attention during the present century, and was a favourite subject of study of the three mathematicians, Cauchy, Hamilton, and Cayley—whom I proceed to mention—though the interests of these writers were by no means limited to this subject.

306. **Cauchy, 1789-1857.** Cauchy was born at Paris, educated at the Polytechnic school, the nursery of so many French mathematicians of that time, and adopted the profession of a civil engineer. In 1816, on the restoration, the French Academy was purged, and, in spite of the contempt of French scientific society, Cauchy accepted a seat procured for him by the expulsion of Monge; he was at the same time made professor at the

Polytechnic. On the revolution in 1830 he went into exile; he returned to France in 1837; and in 1848, and again in 1851 by special dispensation of the emperor, was allowed to occupy a chair of mathematics without taking the oath of allegiance.

307. Among the more important of Cauchy's researches are the discussion of tests for the convergency of series; the determination of the number of real and imaginary roots of any algebraic equation; his method of calculating these roots approximately; his theory of the symmetric functions of the coefficients of equations of any degree; his *à priori* valuation of a quantity less than the least difference between the roots of an equation; and his papers on determinants in 1841, which assisted in bringing them into general use. Cauchy also did something to reduce the art of evaluating definite integrals to a science; but this branch of the integral calculus still remains without much system or method. The rule for finding the principal values of integrals was enunciated by him, and the calculus of residues was his invention. His proof of Taylor's theorem seems to have originated from a discussion of the double periodicity of elliptic functions. The means of shewing a connection between different branches of a subject by giving imaginary values to independent variables is largely due to him. He also gave a direct analytical method for determining planetary inequalities of long period; and to physics he contributed a memoir on the quantity of light reflected from the surfaces of metals, as well as other papers on optics. In many of his memoirs the feverish haste with which they were thrown off is too visible, and several are marred by obscurity, repetition of old results, and blunders.

308. **Hamilton, 1805-1865.** In the opinion of some writers, the *Theory of Quaternions* will be ultimately esteemed one of the great discoveries of this century; that discovery is due to Sir William Rowan Hamilton.

He was born of Scotch parents; in 1824 he entered at
Trinity College, Dublin; his university career is unique,
for the chair of astronomy becoming vacant in 1827,
while he was yet an undergraduate, he was asked by
the electors to stand for it, and was elected unanimously, it being understood that he should be left free
to pursue his own line of study. He occupied this professorship until his death.

309. His earliest researches were on optics. His lectures on quaternions were published in 1852. Amongst
his other papers, I may specially mention one on the
form of the solution of the general algebraic equation of
the fifth degree, which confirmed the conclusion arrived
at by Ruffini and Abel that it cannot be expressed in
terms of the more elementary operations and functions;
one on fluctuating functions; one on the hodograph; and
lastly, one on the numerical solution of differential
equations.

310. **Grassmann, 1809-1877.** The idea of non-commutative algebras and of quaternions seems to have
occurred to Grassmann, professor at Stettin, at about the
same time as to Hamilton. Grassmann's researches on
non-commutative algebras are contained in his *Ausdeh-
nungslehre*, first published in 1844 and enlarged in 1862.
The scientific treatment of the fundamental principles of
algebra, initiated by Hamilton and by Grassmann, was continued by De Morgan and by Boole, and subsequently
was further developed by H. Hankel and by G. Cantor.
Grassmann also investigated the properties of homaloidal
hyper-space.

311. **Cayley, 1821-1895.** Cayley was born near
London, was educated at Cambridge, and was Sadlerian
professor of pure mathematics there from 1863 until his
death. His writings are voluminous, and cover a wide
range of subjects in pure mathematics. His treatment
generally tended to be algebraical, and more than one

critic has pointed out a certain similarity to Euler in the position occupied and the methods adopted.

312. Of his researches I may in particular allude to his ten classical memoirs on quantics (binary and ternary forms), and his researches on non-commutative algebras, especially on matrices. He was the earliest writer to work out the doubly infinite products, and to determine their periodicity; his later researches on elliptic functions dealt mainly with the theory of transformation and the modular equation. He also wrote at length on many problems in and various extensions of analytical geometry, and in particular introduced the so-called "absolute."

313. In *Analytical Geometry* and *Analysis* generally, including therein the Calculus and Differential Equations, the advance during the present century has been as pronounced as in other departments of science, but it is not easy to give a concise sketch of the results arrived at in non-technical language: moreover, much of it is the work of living mathematicians, and as far as possible I avoid in this primer any discussion of their researches.

314. *Modern Synthetic Geometry* may be said to have had its origin in the works of Monge in 1800, Carnot in 1803, and Poncelet in 1822; but these only dimly foreshadowed the great extension it was to receive in Germany, of which Steiner and von Staudt are perhaps the best known exponents.

315. **Steiner, 1796-1863.** Steiner, "the greatest geometrician since the time of Apollonius," was born at Utzensdorf. His father was a peasant, and the boy had no opportunity to learn reading and writing till the age of fourteen. He subsequently went to Heidelberg and thence to Berlin, supporting himself by giving lessons. His researches were embodied in a work published in 1832, which contains a full discussion of the principle of duality, and of the projective and homographic relations of rows, pencils, etc., based on metrical properties. This at once

made his reputation; and a chair of geometry was created for him at Berlin, which he continued to occupy till his death. The most important of his other memoirs relate chiefly to properties of algebraic curves and surfaces, pedals and roulettes, and maxima and minima; the discussion is purely geometrical. Steiner's works may be considered as the classical authority on recent synthetic geometry.

316. **Von Staudt, 1798-1867.** An entirely different system of pure geometry was proposed in 1847 by von Staudt, professor of mathematics at Erlangen. In this he excluded all reference to number or magnitude; but, in spite of its abstract form, he established the non-metrical projective properties of figures, discussed imaginary points, lines, and planes, and even obtained a geometrical definition of a number. This geometry has been used by Culmann as the basis of his graphical statics.

317. Closely connected with the subject of modern geometry is the *Science of Graphics*, in which rules are laid down for solving various problems by the aid of the drawing-board : the modes of calculation which are permissible are considered in modern projective geometry. This method of attacking questions has been hitherto applied chiefly to problems in mechanics, elasticity, and electricity; it is especially useful in engineering, and in that subject an average draughtsman ought to be able to obtain approximate solutions of most of the equations, differential or otherwise, with which he is likely to be concerned, which will not involve errors greater than would have to be allowed for in any case in consequence of our imperfect knowledge of the properties of·the materials employed. The subject has been treated during the last twenty years by numerous writers, especially in Italy and Germany, and applied to a large number of problems.

318. *Theoretical Mechanics, Dynamics, and Astronomy* have

also been of late developed considerably, but the investigations on these subjects cannot be profitably discussed within the limits of this primer, though I must in passing at least mention the names of Bessel (1784-1846), Leverrier (1811-1877), and Adams (1819-1892).

319. *Mathematical Physics.* The history of the recent applications of mathematics to numerous problems in heat, light, elasticity, electricity, and other physical subjects is so extensive that I could not pretend to do it justice, even were its consideration properly included in a history of mathematics: moreover, it is so closely connected with the works of living physicists that I may consider it outside the limits I have laid down for myself. I may, however, note as among the most illustrious physicists of the present century, in addition to those whose researches are indicated in articles above, Green (1793-1841), Clerk Maxwell (1831-1879), von Helmholtz (1821-1894), Sir George Stokes, Lord Kelvin, better known as Sir William Thomson, and Lord Rayleigh. Maxwell's work, in particular, has been far-reaching in its influence on the theories of electricity, magnetism, and light: he discarded the artificial hypotheses previously current, and explained the phenomena by motions and stresses of a single material elastic medium, pervading space and known as the ether.

It is interesting to note that the advance in our knowledge of physics is largely due to the application to it of mathematics, and every year it becomes more difficult for an experimenter to make any mark in the subject unless he is also a mathematician.

Index.

138

NOTE.—The references are to the articles, and not to the pages.

NOTE.—*The references are to the articles, and not to the pages.*

NOTE.—*The references are to the articles, and not to the pages.*

NOTE.—*The references are to the articles, and not to the pages.*

Mercantile Arithmetic, 15n., 111, 140, 147.

Mercator, N., ref. to, 210.

Mersenne, ref. to, 210.

Microscope, Invention of, 215.

Minus; *see* Subtraction.

— Origin of Symbol, 137.

Mohammed, ref. to, 93.

Mohammed ibn Musa; *see* Alkarismi.

Moivre, De, 246.

Monastic Mathematics, 98, 100, 101.

Monge, 274, 306, 314.

Moors, Mathematics of, 117.

Motion, Laws of, 176.

Müller; *see* Regiomontanus.

Multiplication, Symbol for, 170.

Music in the Quadrivium, 12.

Musical Progression, 16.

Napier of Merchistoun, 164-165. ref. to, 168.

Napoleon I., 228, 262, 267, 270.

Negative Sign, 86, 137, 142, 154, 156.

Neil, 202.

Newton, 211-226. ref. to, 50, 56, 60, 76, 156, 176, 181, 184, 185, 189, 209, 210, 231, 238, 239, 246, 249, 253, 261, 276.

Newton's *Principia*, 221-222. ref. to, 209, 245, 253, 266.

Nicole, ref. to, 237.

Non-Euclidean Geometry, 302, 310.

Numbers, Theory of. Treatment of, by Pythagoras, 16; by Euclid, 45-47; by Diophantus, 84, 89; by Fermat, 204; by Euler, 255; by Lagrange, 260; by Legendre, 273; by Gauss, 287, 288; and by other mathematicians of recent times, 293-295, 300, 302.

Numerals, Symbols for, 81, 132, 133.

Numeration, Systems of, 55, 81, 107, 108, 114, 119.

Œnopides of Chios, 19.

Optics (Geometrical). Discussed by (among others) Euclid, 48; Pappus; Roger Bacon; Descartes, 191; Newton, 215; Gauss, 286; and Sir William Hamilton, 309.

— (Physical), 209, 216, 319.

Orrery, 36.

Oughtred, 170.

π, value of, 55, 71.

Pacioli, 138-143.

Pappus, 74-76. ref. to, 189.

Parabola, area of, 55, 194.

Parmenides, 20.

Pascal, 195-199. ref. to, 156, 202, 206, 274.

Peacock, ref. to, 281.

Pendulum, 174, 208.

Perspective, 247.

Philolaus, 11.

Phoenician Mathematics, 3.

Physics, Mathematical, 275, 319; also *see* headings of subjects.

Picard, ref. to, 218.

Planetary Motions, 36, 64, 71, 177, 182, 220, 221, 265, 285, 290.

Plato, 31-33. ref. to, 11, 25, 41.

Plus, Symbols for, 86, 137, 142, 154, 156.

Plutarch, ref. to, 5.

Poisson, 277-279.

Poles and Polars; *see* Geometry (Modern Synthetic).

Polyhedrons, Regular, 14.

Poncelet, ref. to, 274, 314.

Potential, 260, 265, 273.

Powers; *see* Exponents.

Pretender, the Young, 248.

Primes, Theory of, 16, 46, 61.

— Distribution of, 293, 302.

Principia; *see* Newton.

Printing, Invention of, 131, 134, 144.

Probabilities, 198, 206, 234, 246, 253, 268, 273, 279, 284.

Product, Symbol for, 170.

Progressions, 16.

NOTE.—*The references are to the articles, and not to the pages.*

NOTE.—*The references are to the articles, and not to the pages.*

GLASGOW : PRINTED AT THE UNIVERSITY PRESS BY ROBERT MACLEHOSE AND CO.

A SHORT ACCOUNT OF THE

HISTORY OF MATHEMATICS.

BY W. W. ROUSE BALL.

[Second Edition. Pp. xxiv + 520. *Price* 10s. *net.]*

MACMILLAN AND CO., LONDON AND NEW YORK.

THIS book gives an account of the lives and discoveries of those mathematicians to whom the development of the subject is mainly due. The use of technicalities has been avoided, and the work is intelligible to any one acquainted with the elements of mathematics.

The author commences with an account of the origin and progress of Greek mathematics, from which the Alexandrian, the Indian, and the Arab schools may be said to have arisen. Next the mathematics of mediæval Europe and the renaissance are described. The latter part of the book is devoted to the history of modern mathematics (beginning with the invention of analytical geometry and the infinitesimal calculus), the account of which is brought down to the present time.

This excellent summary of the history of mathematics supplies a want which has long been felt in this country. The extremely difficult question, how far such a work should be technical, has been solved with great tact. . . . The work contains many valuable hints, and is thoroughly readable. The biographies, which include those of most of the men who played important parts in the development of culture, are full and general enough to interest the ordinary reader as well as the specialist. Its value to the latter is much increased by the numerous references to authorities, a good table of contents, and a full and accurate index.—*The Saturday Review.*

Mr. Ball's book should meet with a hearty welcome, for though we possess other histories of special branches of mathematics, this is the first serious attempt that has been made in the English language to give a systematic account of the origin and development of the science as a whole. It is written too in an attractive style. Technicalities are not too numerous or obtrusive, and the work is interspersed with biographical sketches and anecdotes likely to interest the general reader. Thus the tyro and the advanced mathematician alike may read it with pleasure and profit.—*The Athenæum.*

148

A wealth of authorities, often far from accordant with each other, renders a work such as this extremely formidable ; and students of mathematics have reason to be grateful for the vast amount of information which has been condensed into this short account. . . . In a survey of so wide extent it is of course impossible to give anything but a bare sketch of the various lines of research, and this circumstance tends to render a narrative scrappy. It says much for Mr. Ball's descriptive skill that his history reads more like a continuous story than a series of merely consecutive summaries. — *The Academy.*

We can heartily recommend to our mathematical readers, and to others also, Mr. Ball's *History of Mathematics.* The history of what might be supposed a dry subject is told in the pleasantest and most readable style, and at the same time there is evidence of the most careful research. — *The Observatory.*

All the salient points of mathematical history are given, and many of the results of recent antiquarian research ; but it must not be imagined that the book is at all dry. On the contrary the biographical sketches frequently contain amusing anecdotes, and many of the theorems mentioned are very clearly explained so as to bring them within the grasp of those who are only acquainted with elementary mathematics.—*Nature.*

Le style de M. Ball est clair et élégant, de nombreux aperçus rendent facile de suivre le fil de son exposition et de fréquentes citations permettent à celui qui le désire d'approfondir les recherches que l'auteur n'a pu qu'effleurer. . . . Cet ouvrage pourra devenir très utile comme manuel d'histoire des mathématiques pour les étudiants, et il ne sera pas déplacé dans les bibliothèques des savants.—*Bibliotheca Mathematica.*

The author modestly describes his work as a compilation, but it is thoroughly well digested, a due proportion is observed between the various parts, and when occasion demands he does not hesitate to give an independent judgment on a disputed point. His verdicts in such instances appear to us to be generally sound and reasonable. . . . To many readers who have not the courage or the opportunity to tackle the ponderous volumes of Montucla or the (mostly) ponderous treatises of German writers on special periods, it may be somewhat of a surprise to find what a wealth of human interest attaches to the history of so "dry" a subject as mathematics. We are brought into contact with many remarkable men, some of whom have played a great part in other fields, as the names of Gerbert, Wren, Leibnitz, Descartes, Pascal, D'Alembert, Carnot, among others may testify, and with at least one thorough blackguard (Cardan); and Mr. Ball's pages abound with quaint and amusing touches characteristic of the authors under consideration, or of the times in which they lived.—*Manchester Guardian.*

There can be no doubt that the author has done his work in a very excellent way. . . . There is no one interested in almost any part of mathematical science who will not welcome such an exposition as the present, at once popularly written and exact, embracing the entire subject. . . . Mr. Ball's work is destined to become a standard one on the subject.--*The Glasgow Herald.*

MATHEMATICAL
RECREATIONS AND PROBLEMS.

By W. W. ROUSE BALL.

[Second Edition. Pp. xii + 241. *Price 7s. net.]*

MACMILLAN AND CO., LONDON AND NEW YORK.

THIS work is divided into two parts, the first on mathematical recreations and puzzles, the second on some problems of historical interest; but in both parts questions which involve advanced mathematics are excluded.

The mathematical recreations include numerous elementary questions, as well as problems such as the proposition that to colour a map not more than four colours are necessary, the explanation of the possibility of sailing quicker than the wind, the effect of a cut on a tennis ball, the fifteen puzzle, Chinese rings, the eight queens problem, the fifteen school-girls, the construction of magic squares, the theory and history of mazes and similar figures, the Hamiltonian game, and the knight's path on a chess-board.

The second part commences with a sketch of the history, first, of three classical problems in geometry—namely, the duplication of the cube, the trisection of an angle, and the quadrature of the circle—and second, of astrology. The last three chapters are devoted to an account of the hypotheses as to the nature of space and mass, and the means of measuring time.

Mr. Ball has already attained a position in the front rank of writers on subjects connected with the history of mathematics, and this brochure will add another to his successes in this field. In it he has collected a mass of information bearing upon matters of more general interest, written in a style which is eminently readable, and at the same time exact. He has done his work so thoroughly that he has left few ears for other gleaners. The nature of the work is completely indicated to the mathematical student by its title. Does he want to revive his acquaintance with the *Problèmes Plaisans et Délectables* of Bachet or the *Récréations Mathématiques et Physiques* of Ozanam? Let him take Mr. Ball for his companion, and he will have the cream of these works put before him with a wealth of illustration quite delightful. Or, coming to more recent times, he will have full and accurate discussion of 'the fifteen puzzle,' 'Chinese rings,' 'the fifteen school-girls problem,' *et id genus omne*. Sufficient space is devoted to accounts of magic squares and unicursal problems (such as mazes, the knight's path, and geometrical trees). These, and many other problems of equal interest, come under the head of 'Recreations.' The problems and speculations include an account of the Three Classical Problems; there is also a brief sketch of Astrology; and interesting outlines of the present state of our knowledge of hyper-space and of the constitution of matter. This enumeration baldly indicates the matter handled, but it sufficiently states what the reader may expect to find. Moreover, for the use of readers who may wish to pursue the several heads further, Mr. Ball gives detailed references to the sources from whence he has derived his information. These *Mathematical Recreations* we can commend as suited for mathematicians and equally for others who wish to while away an occasional hour.—*The Academy.*

The idea of writing some such account as that before us must have been present to Mr. Ball's mind when he was collecting the material which he has so skilfully worked up into his *History of Mathematics.* We think this because the extent of ground covered by these *Recreations* is commensurate with that of the *History*, and many bits of ore which would not suit the earlier work find a fitting niche in this. Howsoever the case may be, we are sure that non-mathematical, as well as mathematical, readers will derive amusement, and, we venture to think, profit withal, from a perusal of it. The author has gone very exhaustively over the ground, and has left us little opportunity of adding to or correcting what he has thus reproduced from his note-books. The work before us is divided into two parts: mathematical recreations and mathematical problems and speculations. All these matters are treated lucidly, and with sufficient detail for the ordinary reader, and for others there is ample store of references. . . . Our analysis shows how great an extent of ground is covered by the *Mathematical Recreations*, and when we add that the account is fully pervaded by the attractive charm Mr. Ball knows so well how to infuse into what many persons would look upon as a dry subject, we have said all we can to commend it to our readers.— *Nature.*

A fit sequel to its author's valuable and interesting works on the history of mathematics. There is a fascination about this volume which results from a happy combination of puzzle and paradox. There is both milk for babes

·and strong meat for grown men. . . . A great deal of the information is hardly accessible in any English books; and Mr. Ball would deserve the gratitude of mathematicians for having merely collected the facts. But he has presented them with such lucidity and vivacity of style that there is not a dull page in the book; and he has added minute and full bibliographical references which greatly enhance the value of his work.—*The Cambridge Review.*

Mathematicians with a turn for the paradoxes and puzzles connected with number, space, and time, in which their science abounds, will delight in *Mathematical Recreations and Problems of Past and Present Times.*—*The Times.*

Mathematicians have their recreations; and Mr. Ball sets forth the humours of mathematics in a book of deepest interest to the clerical reader, and of no little attractiveness to the layman. The notes attest an enormous amount of research.—*The National Observer.*

Mathematical Recreations and Problems contains, as its title suggests, an account of certain mathematical amusements and speculations of past and present times; some of them of historic interest, and some gathered from the latest papers of Cayley and Darwin. Mr. Ball hastens to warn his reader that "the conclusions are of no practical use, and most of the results are not new." But in spite of that, the book is one that may be read both for amusement and profit; and although the versed mathematician will be most at home with some of its reasonings, yet the reader with a mere smattering of numbers can extract much nutriment from Mr. Ball's lucid presentation and explanation of the questions that many wise heads have puzzled over. . . . Take it all round, Mr. Ball has produced a book of extreme and all but unique interest to general readers who dabble in science as well as to professed mathematicians.—*The Scottish Leader.*

Mr. Ball, to whom we are already indebted for two excellent Histories of Mathematics, has just produced a book which will be thoroughly appreciated by those who enjoy the setting of the wits to work. . . . He has collected a vast amount of information about mathematical quips, tricks, cranks, and puzzles—old and new; and it will be strange if even the most learned do not find something fresh in the assortment.—*The Observatory.*

Mr. Rouse Ball has the true gift of story-telling, and he writes so pleasantly that though we enjoy the fulness of his knowledge we are tempted to forget the considerable amount of labour involved in the preparation of his book. He gives us the history and the mathematics of many problems . . . and where the limits of his work prevent him from dealing fully with the points raised, like a true worker he gives us ample references to original memoirs. . . . The book is warmly to be recommended, and should find a place on the shelves of everyone interested in mathematics and on those of every public library.—*The Manchester Guardian.*

Those furnished with not much more knowledge of mathematics than forms part of an ordinary education will find much to interest them in Mr. Ball's volume, which will open up to them much that in ordinary form is beyond their reach. . . . Mr. Ball's explanations are all clear and suggestive, and the book is one which is calculated to arouse in many a dormant taste for mathematics.—*The Scotsman.*

A work which will interest all who delight in mathematics and mental exercises generally. The student will often take it up, as it contains many problems which puzzle even clever people.—*The English Mechanic and World of Science.*

This is a book which the general reader should find as interesting as the mathematician. At all events, an intelligent enjoyment of its contents presupposes no more knowledge of mathematics than is now-a-days possessed by almost everybody.—*The Athenæum.*

Once more the author of a *Short History of Mathematics* and a *History of the Study of Mathematics at Cambridge* gives evidence of the width of his reading and of his skill in compilation. From the elementary arithmetical puzzles which were known in the sixteenth and seventeenth centuries to those modern ones, the mathematical discussion of which has taxed the energies of the ablest investigator, very few questions have been left unrepresented. The sources of the author's information are indicated with great fulness. . . . The book is a welcome addition to English mathematical literature.—*The Oxford Magazine.*

A book which deserves to be widely known by those who are fond of solving puzzles . . . and will be found to contain an admirable classified collection of ingenious questions capable of mathematical analysis. As the author is himself a skilful mathematician, and is careful to add an analysis of most of the propositions, it may easily be believed that there is food for study as well as amusement in his pages. . . . Is in every way worthy of praise.—*The School Guardian.*

The work is a very judicious and suggestive compilation, not meant mainly for mathematicians, yet made doubly valuable to them by copious references. The style in the main is so compact and clear that what is central in a long argument or process is admirably presented in a few words. One great merit of this, or any other really good book on such a subject, is its suggestiveness; and in running through its pages, one is pretty sure to think of additional problems on the same general lines.—*Bulletin of the New York Mathematical Society.*

To the mathematician especially this will be a most welcome book.—*The Glasgow Herald.*

The book is very interesting, and judiciously combines instruction and recreation.—*The Educational Times.*

Eine Fülle angenehmer Unterhaltung.—*Jahrbuch über die Fortschritte der Mathematik.*

A HISTORY OF THE STUDY OF
MATHEMATICS AT CAMBRIDGE.

By W. W. ROUSE BALL.

[*Pp.* xvi + 264.   *Price* 6*s.*]

THE UNIVERSITY PRESS, CAMBRIDGE.

This work contains an account of the development of the study of mathematics in the University of Cambridge from the twelfth century to the middle of the nineteenth century, and a description of the means by which proficiency in that study was tested at various times.

The first part of the book is devoted to an enumeration of the more eminent Cambridge mathematicians, arranged chronologically: the subject-matter of their more important works is stated, and the methods of exposition which they used are indicated. Any reader who may wish to omit details will find a description of the characteristic features of each period in the introductory paragraphs of the chapter concerning it.

The second part of the book treats of the manner in which mathematics was taught, and of the exercises and examinations required of students in successive generations. To explain the relation of mathematics to other departments of study a brief outline of the general history of the university and of the organization of education therein is added.

The present volume is very pleasant reading, and though much of it necessarily appeals only to mathematicians, there are parts—*e.g.* the chapters on Newton, on the growth of the tripos, and on the history of the university —which are full of interest for a general reader. . . . The book is well written, the style is crisp and clear, and there is a humorous appreciation of some of the curious old regulations which have been superseded by time and change of custom. Though it seems light, it must represent an extensive study and investigation on the part of the author, the essential results of which are skilfully given. We can most thoroughly commend Mr. Ball's

154

volume to all readers who are interested in mathematics or in the growth and the position of the Cambridge school of mathematicians.—*The Manchester Guardian.*

Voici un livre dont la lecture inspire tout d'abord le regret que des travaux analogues n'aient pas été faits pour toutes les Écoles célèbres, et avec autant de soin et de clarté. . . . Toutes les parties du livre nous ont vivement intéressé.—*Bulletin des sciences mathématiques.*

A book of pleasant and useful reading for both historians and mathematicians. Mr. Ball's previous researches into this kind of history have already established his reputation, and the book is worthy of the reputation of its author. It is more than a detailed account of the rise and progress of mathematics, for it involves a very exact history of the University of Cambridge from its foundation.—*The Educational Times.*

Mr Ball is far from confining his narrative to the particular science of which he is himself an acknowledged master, and his account of the study of mathematics becomes a series of biographical portraits of eminent professors and a record not only of the intellectual life of the *élite* but of the manners, habits, and discussions of the great body of Cambridge men from the sixteenth century to our own.—*The Daily News.*

Mr. Ball has not only given us a detailed account of the rise and progress of the science with which the name of Cambridge is generally associated, but has also written a brief but reliable and interesting history of the university itself from its foundation down to recent times. . . . The book is pleasant reading alike for the mathematician and the student of history.—*St. James's Gazette.*

A very handy and valuable book containing, as it does, a vast deal of interesting information which could not without inconceivable trouble be found elsewhere. . . . It is very far from forming merely a mathematical biographical dictionary, the growth of mathematical science being skilfully traced in connection with the successive names. There are probably very few people who will be able thoroughly to appreciate the author's laborious researches in all sorts of memoirs and transactions of learned societies in order to unearth the material which he has so agreeably condensed. . . . Along with this there is much new matter which, while of great interest to mathematicians, and more especially to men brought up at Cambridge, will be found to throw a good deal of new and important light on the history of education in general.—*The Glasgow Herald.*

Exceedingly interesting to all who care for mathematics.—*The Literary World.*

The book is very enjoyable, and gives a capital and accurate digest of many excellent authorities which are not within the reach of the ordinary reader.—*The Scots Observer.*

AN ESSAY ON

THE GENESIS, CONTENTS, AND HISTORY OF

NEWTON'S "PRINCIPIA."

BY W. W. ROUSE BALL.

[*Pp.* x + 175.   *Price* 6s.   *net.*]

MACMILLAN AND CO., LONDON AND NEW YORK.

THIS work contains an account of the successive discoveries of Newton on gravitation, the methods he used, and the history of his researches. It commences with a review of the extant authorities dealing with the subject. In the next two chapters the investigations made in 1666 and 1679 are discussed, some of the documents dealing therewith being here printed for the first time. The fourth chapter is devoted to the investigations made in 1684: these are illustrated by Newton's professorial lectures (of which the original manuscript is extant) of that autumn, and are summed up in the almost unknown memoir of February, 1685, which is here reproduced from Newton's holograph copy. In the two following chapters the details of the preparation from 1685 to 1687 of the *Principia* are described, and an analysis of the work is given. The seventh chapter comprises an account of the researches of Newton on gravitation subsequent to the publication of the first edition of the *Principia*, and a sketch of the history of that work. In the last chapter, the extant letters of 1678-1679 between Hooke and Newton, and of those of 1686-1687 between Halley and Newton are reprinted, and there are also notes on the extant correspondence concerning the production of the second and third editions of the *Principia*.

For the essay which we have before us, Mr. Ball should receive the thanks of all those to whom the name of Newton recalls the memory of a great man. The *Principia*, besides being a lasting monument of Newton's life, is also to-day the classic of our mathematical writings, and will be so for some time to come. . . . The value of the present work is also enhanced by the fact that, besides containing a few as yet unpublished letters, there are collected in its pages quotations from all documents, thus forming a complete summary of everything that is known on the subject. . . . The author is so well-known a writer on anything connected with the history of mathematics, that we need make no mention of the thoroughness of the essay, while it would be superfluous for us to add that from beginning to end it is pleasantly written and delightful to read. Those well acquainted with the *Principia* will find much that will interest them, while those not so fully enlightened will learn much by reading through this account of the origin and history of Newton's greatest work.—*Nature.*

An Essay on Newton's Principia will suggest to many something solely mathematical, and therefore wholly uninteresting. No inference could be more erroneous. The book certainly deals largely in scientific technicalities which will interest experts only; but it also contains much historical information which might attract many who, from laziness or inability, would be very willing to take all its mathematics for granted. Mr. Ball carefully examines the evidence bearing on the development of Newton's great discovery, and supplies the reader with abundant quotations from contemporary authorities. Not the least interesting portion of the book is the appendix, or rather appendices, containing copies of the original documents (mostly letters) to which Mr. Ball refers in his historical criticisms.—*The Athenæum.*

La savante monographie de M. Ball est rédigée avec beaucoup de soin, et à plusiers égards elle peut servir de modèle pour des écrits de la même nature.—*Bibliotheca Mathematica.*

Newton's *Principia* has world-wide fame as a classic of mathematical science. But those who know thoroughly the contents and the history of the book are a select company. It was at one time the purpose of Mr. Ball to prepare a new critical edition of the work, accompanied by a prefatory history and notes, and by an analytical commentary. Mathematicians will regret to hear that there is no prospect in the immediate future of seeing this important book carried to completion by so competent a hand. They will at the same time welcome Mr. Ball's *Essay on the Principia* for the elucidations which it gives of the process by which Newton's great work originated and took form, and also as an earnest of the completed plan.—*The Scotsman.*

In this essay Mr. Ball presents us with an account highly interesting to mathematicians and natural philosophers of the origin and history of that remarkable product of a great genius, *Philosophiae Naturalis Principia Mathematica*, 'The Mathematical Principles of Natural Philosophy,' better known by the short term *Principia.* . . . Mr. Ball's essay is one of extreme interest to students of physical science, and it is sure to be widely read and greatly appreciated.—*The Glasgow Herald.*

To his well-known and scholarly treatises on the *History of Mathematics*
Mr. W. W. Rouse Ball has added *An Essay on Newton's Principia*. Newton's
Principia, as Mr. Ball justly observes, is the classic of English mathematical
writings; and this sound, luminous, and laborious essay ought to be the
classical account of the *Principia*. The essay is the outcome of a critical
edition of Newton's great work, which Mr. Ball tells us that he once con-
templated. It is much to be hoped that he will carry out his intention, for
no English mathematician is likely to do the work better or in a more
reverent spirit. . . . It is unnecessary to say that Mr. Ball has a complete knowledge of his subject. He writes with an ease and clearness that
are rare.—*The Scottish Leader*.

Le volume de M. Rouse Ball renferme tout ce que l'on peut désirer savoir
sur l'histoire des *Principes*; c'est d'ailleurs l'œuvre d'un esprit clair, judicieux,
et méthodique.—*Bulletin des Sciences Mathématiques*.

Mr. Ball has put into small space a very great deal of interesting matter,
and his book ought to meet with a wide circulation among lovers of Newton
and the *Principia*.—*The Academy*.

Admirers of Mr. W. W. Rouse Ball's *Short Account of the History of
Mathematics* will be glad to receive a detailed study of the history of the
Principia from the same hand. This book, like its predecessor, gives a very
lucid account of its subject. . . . Probably the part of the book which
will be found most interesting by the general reader is the account of the
correspondence of Newton with Hooke, and with Halley, about the contents
or the publication of the *Principia*. This correspondence is given in full, so
far as it is recoverable. Hooke does not appear to advantage in it. He
accuses Newton of stealing his ideas. His vain and envious disposition made
his own merits appear great in his eyes, and be-dwarfed the work of others,
so that he seems to have believed that Newton's great performance was a
mere expanding and editing of the ideas of Mr. Hooke—ideas which were
meritorious, but after all mere guesses at truth. This, at all events, is the
most charitable view we can take of his conduct. Halley, on the contrary,
appears as a man to whom we ought to feel most grateful. It almost seems
as though Newton's physical insight and extraordinary mathematical powers
might have been largely wasted, as was Pascal's rare genius, if it had not been
for Halley's single-hearted and self-forgetful efforts to get from his friends'
genius all he could for the enlightenment of men. It was probably at his
suggestion that the writing of the *Principia* was undertaken. When the
work was presented to the Royal Society, they undertook its publication, but,
being without the necessary funds, the expense fell upon Halley. When
Newton, stung by Hooke's accusations, wished to withdraw a part of the
work, Halley's tact was required to avert the catastrophe. All the drudgery,

worry, and expense fell to his share, and was accepted with the most generous good nature. It will be seen that both the technical student and the general reader may find much to interest him in Mr. Rouse Ball's book.—*The Manchester Guardian.*

Une histoire très bien faite de la genèse du livre immortel de Newton. . . . Le livre de M. Ball est une monographie précieuse sur un point important de l'histoire des mathématiques. Il contribuera à accroître, si c'est possible, la gloire de Newton, en révélant à beaucoup de lectures, avec quelle marveilleuse rapidité l'illustre géométre anglais a élevé à la science ce monument immortel, les *Principia.*—*Mathesis.*

CPSIA information can be obtained
at www.ICGtesting.com
Printed in the USA
LVHW081628200921
698273LV00010B/437